WISE
DECISIONS

WISE
DECISIONS

A SCIENCE-BASED APPROACH TO
MAKING BETTER CHOICES

DR. JIM LOEHR | DR. SHEILA OHLSSON

WILEY

For general information on our other products and services or for technical support, please
contact our Customer Care Department within the United States at (800) 762-2974, outside
the United States at (317) 572-3993 or fax (317) 572-4002.

Wiley also publishes its books in a variety of electronic formats. Some content that appears in
print may not be available in electronic formats. For more information about Wiley products,
visit our web site at www.wiley.com.

Library of Congress Cataloging-in-Publication Data:

Names: Loehr, Jim, author. | Ohlsson, Sheila, author.
Title: Wise decisions : a science-based approach to making better choices /
   Dr. James E Loehr and Dr. Sheila Ohlsson Walker.
Description: Hoboken, New Jersey : Wiley, [2023] | Includes bibliographical
   references and index.
Identifiers: LCCN 2022029667 (print) | LCCN 2022029668 (ebook) | ISBN
   9781119931409 (hardback) | ISBN 9781119931423 (adobe pdf) | ISBN
   9781119931416 (epub)
Subjects: LCSH: Decision making.
Classification: LCC HD30.23 .L635 2023 (print) | LCC HD30.23 (ebook) |
   DDC 658.4/03—dc23/eng/20220811
LC record available at https://lccn.loc.gov/2022029667
LC ebook record available at https://lccn.loc.gov/2022029668

Cover Art: © ZOART STUDIO / GETTY IMAGES
Cover Design: PAUL McCARTHY

SKY10036858_101922

To my seven grandchildren, Wes, Ced, Theo, Archie, Riley, Jack, and Max. May they demonstrate in their lives what wise decision-making really means.
—Jim

To my three beautiful sons, Jack, Charlie, and Wyatt. May they embody wisdom, kindness, empathy, and purpose in decision-making across their lives.
—Sheila

CONTENTS

FOREWORD

This is the first book foreword I've ever written, and I do so at the age of 90 because I wholeheartedly believe its pages hold life-changing wisdom and perspective. *Wise Decisions* contains something not just for certain people, but all people, because it's our everyday decisions, whether large or small, that ultimately determine how we show up in life.

The pages ahead lay out a roadmap for building and strengthening our decision-making capacities, supporting us in making the kinds of choices that stand the test of time. Importantly, walking our talk with the young people in our lives, whether our children, students, athletes, grandchildren, or simply multigenerational friends, teaches them by example how to make thoughtful, intentional choices, offering them a priceless gift that will shape their life trajectories in unforeseeable yet powerful ways across time.

As I read through this book for the first time, I reflected more deeply on the people and experiences that shaped my own decision-making process, and what became clear was simply this: just about everything I needed to know about making wise and thoughtful choices was taught to me by my grandfather during childhood hikes in the mountains of North Carolina.

Despite being an outsized force in our community, my grandfather embodied the values of kindness, respect, integrity, and service always and without exception. Not once did I see him display arrogance, anger, or act in a demanding way. He showed up for others, whether it was a close friend or a stranger from one of the nearby poverty-ridden farming communities, and when a tough decision needed to be made, his inner guidance was plain and simple—he did the right thing.

My grandfather's actions spoke volumes, as a steadfast rule choosing the hard right over the easy wrong. Having built and funded the first school for African American children in China Grove, North

Carolina, years before I was born, his ethic of caring, respect, and support for others, regardless of their circumstances, were the defining traits by which he was known in our community and our church. He was a true leader in every possible way, his values and ideals playing out in real time in the tangible decisions he made that impacted lives for the better.

All of this took root in me in a way I can see more clearly now in hindsight, the cutting-edge science of how I became who I am today illuminated across the science-focused chapters of this book. The bottom line is that it was both *what he did* and *how he did it* that stuck with me over time. As I think back, I remember how he respected and trusted me, spoke with me much like an adult despite being only five years old, and gave me opportunities to think deeply and reflect, to engage with him in the process of making decisions.

His unending care and respect wove a thread through interactions with myself and others, indelibly shaping the man I grew up to be. He instilled in me a sense that my ideas, thoughts, emotions, and questions had merit. He infused in me a sense of value for the important things in life, not material goods, but rather service to others and making our world better in a way that I uniquely could. He showed me how I too could navigate my own path in life such that, like him, I could impact the lives of others in a positive way. Just by walking his talk, he instilled in me a decision-making framework that has always felt like second nature, just a part of who I am.

This insight reinforced in an even deeper way the extraordinary capacity of adults to shape the minds, bodies, and higher-order spiritual beliefs of young people. And it's the times when emotions are running high, so-called "teachable moments," when the most powerful opportunities to lead by example present themselves. These are the rare moments within the fertile soil of a safe, trusted, and respectful relationship, when we adults can embed powerful life lessons that provide a felt sense of confidence, competence, and purpose for the young people we want, over and above all else, to see flourish.

Without question, this is the priceless gift my grandfather gave to me.

Prior to reading this book I'd never thought in considerable detail about the components of how I've made decisions. Nor had I ever tried to take the process from inside the black box of my mind and put it into words. Having now done this, a few things stand out.

First, my health, exercising every day, eating healthy food, and getting a good night's sleep is and always has been fundamental for the clear thinking I've needed to make solid decisions. The ways in which health ignites wise decision-making is the topic of the book's lead chapter. Second, while the concrete facts of any issue are important for thoughtful and informed deliberation, I now see the magnitude to which trusting the wisdom of my body, via my emotions and intuition, have played a role in the decisions I've made. I saw my grandfather do this over and over and recognize that these same core qualities have become second nature. Third, when I have a big decision to make, the solitude and freedom of nature helps me see the bigger picture more clearly, a particularly relevant fact in this era of relentless exposure to screens and social media. And fourth, if I was to lay out my decision-making process, I'd say it's been a combination of hard data and "gut feel", with input from a handful of wise friends, that have guided me throughout my 91 years. Incidentally, my body's language of emotion and intuition often provided clearer and more immediate feedback than the back-and-forth of hypothetical outcomes unfolding in my brain, all which set the stage to channel the ethos of my grandfather: to do the right thing.

Of the hard decisions I've had to make in life, whether in business as chairman of Westinghouse Broadcasting faced with mafia-driven death threats, making the call in 1981 to break the Acquired Immune Deficiency Syndrome (AIDS) story to the world, or as Chancellor of the University of Denver, the spirit of my grandfather has run a thread through them all.

At age 58 I'd retired from Westinghouse and had planned to live my remaining days as a cowboy on my ranch in Colorado. Out of the blue one day, a dear friend posed a question I'd never anticipated in a million years, whether I'd take over as Chancellor at the University of Denver. Not believing I had the capacity nor the skill set, especially at a university that was in significant trouble, I nonetheless chose to vet the idea with three close wise friends, who to a tee endorsed the idea.

It was a brand-new challenge, and I decided to take it on, just for a short few-year stint, to help the university stabilize and find new leadership. Sixteen years later, much to my surprise, I'd fallen head over heels in love with DU, most powerfully with the opportunity to shape young lives in a profoundly impactful way.

With the support and collaboration of an incredible team of trusted, creative, passionate and purposeful women and men, DU took on a whole new life. We were forced to make many hard decisions across time, letting go of long-standing employees who didn't uphold basic standards of ethical behavior, all at a time when the university was bleeding financially, and student enrollment was on the decline. Decision by decision, we moved in the direction of True North, and slowly but surely, we began to turn a corner.

Together we introduced and enforced rigorous standards around character and integrity across academics and athletics, upheld the core principles of kindness and service to others, and maintained an overarching focus on developing and graduating students of honor, integrity, and purpose who had the healthy bodies, minds, hearts, and souls to go out and change our world. Like my grandfather, it was vital that we modeled what we expected of others as we worked to reshape the culture and emotional climate of the university. This required making many hard choices along the way.

One in particular stands out because I love sports, and this story is emblazoned in my memory. In April 2004 the DU men's hockey team was in the finals of the NCAA Division I championship game in Boston, and odds were stacked in favor of the other team. The night before the highly anticipated game, one of DU's star players, a top scorer and the one who had made the go-ahead goal in the semifinal game, had violated the standards of behavior required to take the ice with his team the following day. In a difficult and time-sensitive conversation between myself, the Athletic Director and the head coach, we needed to make a call, all the while knowing his absence on the ice in the final meant not only lower odds of a win, but more importantly, a lesser chance of the ripple effect of all that a Division 1 championship win would mean for DU as an institution.

On game day, as DU took the ice against their rivals, the young man lived out the consequences of his character infraction. The stalwart player was not included in the lineup, but rather sat in the stands, dressed in a suit and tie, with teammates who were injured or hadn't made the 20 player roster. The message: Whether a star or second-string freshman, all players live by the same system of rules and receive the same penalties for noncompliance. It was a vibrant living example of what DU stood for, representative of the culture we'd intentionally and carefully cultivated over time. On a joyful closing note that further validated our decision to stand by our principles, DU won the NCAA championship in a game that, up till the final seconds, could have gone either way.

On the surface we had to make a hard decision, but asking the simple question "What's the right thing to do?" made the answer clear as day.

If I had to pick one part of my life for which I feel the deepest gratitude across my 91 years, it is my time at DU. I worked harder than ever before, intrinsically motivated by shaping young lives with my team, fueled by being able to provide insight and guidance on their life journeys. This job, more than any others, pushed my decision-making process like never before. And the payoff, that of helping young people write their stories of passion and purpose, is beyond anything that can be quantified monetarily.

While not all decisions were perfect nor played out as planned, when it came right down to the nuts and bolts, it was because of the higher-order principles, something this book calls "the spiritual dimension," that I was able to stay clear on the path forward. My grandfather's words "Do the right thing" were at the very core of my process.

Wise Decisions will help you make the kinds of choices that support you and those you love in charting a course through life that you are proud of, a journey of substance and contribution. Its guidance, if you choose to follow it, will improve your health, strengthen your relationships, and connect you with the sense of purpose and wisdom that fuels your mind and body, aligned with the values and beliefs most meaningful to you. Moreover, speaking with your actions, in particular living your "why," will help you capitalize on a timely opportunity to redefine what it means to be human in our world today. All during a period in our world history that calls for kindness, integrity, generosity, gratitude, humility, and courage in our leaders and global society more than ever.

—Dan Ritchie

Dan Ritchie is the former CEO of Westinghouse Broadcasting, chancellor of the University of Denver for 16 years, and former chairman and CEO of the Denver Center for Performing Arts. He received the inaugural Colorado Governor's Medal in 2015 for strengthening Colorado communities, and was president of the Temple Hoyne Buell Foundation, a pioneer in supporting early childhood education, for over two decades.

Introduction

L et's face it: Human beings are flawed decision makers. The corporate world is replete with examples: Blockbuster Video rejected Netflix; Kodak could have become the next Apple had the leadership made better decisions; Excite could have purchased Google for $750,000; Ross Perot passed on Microsoft; Motorola decided against smartphones; DECCA records turned down the Beatles, and on and on. And then there are the catastrophic examples of faulty decision-making at Enron, Arthur Anderson, WorldCom, and Halliburton, to mention just a few. And how about Congress? The approval rating of Congress, according to Gallup in January 2022, was only 18%! Put another way, 82% of those polled disagree with the decisions made by Congress.

The data on personal finance decisions is equally disturbing. Eight percent of all people who file for bankruptcy have filed at least once before and 5% of bankruptcy cases are attributed to reckless spending. Well-educated people file 20% of American bankruptcies. It is estimated that 14 million Americans have over $10,000 of credit card debt. The CDC's National Center for Health Statistics reports that 42% of all marriages result in divorce. The combination of four healthy lifestyle choices—maintaining a healthy weight, exercising regularly, following a healthy diet, and not smoking—are associated with an 80% reduction in the risk of developing chronic diseases but, in spite of the evidence, large numbers of well-informed people continue to make bad health decisions. And let's not overlook the all-too-frequent poor decision-making in the sports world: doping and cycling, illegal drug use and swimming, gambling and baseball, and the NFL's Spygate and Deflategate. In the soccer scandal involving its own federation (FIFA), 14 people were indicted in connection with bribery charges.

In all these examples and countless others, people's decision-making processes failed them. Whatever vetting process was deployed simply wasn't good enough, resulting in sometimes catastrophic outcomes.

DECISION FATIGUE

Do I stay up late and watch a movie or go to bed now? Do I call home tonight or wait until tomorrow? Do I get up 45 minutes earlier and work out before going to work? Should I skip breakfast because I'm running late? Should I say what I really think or keep my mouth shut? Should I give the guy holding a "homeless" sign five dollars? It's snowing; should I pick my son up at school or have my ex-husband do it? Should we sell our home and move out of the city? Should we go into debt to pay for our daughter's college? I hate my job! Should I quit? I think our son is sleeping with his girlfriend; should I confront him even though I have no real evidence? Should I go to the party tonight or drive to see my ailing mother? Should I have a burger or a taco? Should I get gas now or later? Should I buy bananas or oranges?

In a span of 15 minutes, we can make 10 or more such decisions. Some decisions are inconsequential and others can change the trajectory of our lives forever. Reflect for a moment on the decisions you made in your life, both good and bad, that had real consequences. Consider how a single decision you made changed everything going forward. Just as success in business depends on the decisions made, so also does enduring success in our personal lives. Decisions can be wise or foolish, considered or automatic, conscious or unconscious, emotional or rational, reasonable or unreasonable.

Some poor decisions can be traced to something called *choice overload*, meaning too many options, decisions, and choices. All decision-making consumes energy, and the more we care about the outcome, the more our bodies expend energy (e.g. accelerated heart rate). Eventually, our mental and emotional energy reserves become depleted with the consequence of hitting the proverbial *decision-making wall*. As will be pointed out repeatedly throughout this book and particularly in

Chapter 11, strategically using rest, physical movement, nutritional intake, and hydration can quickly replenish energy reserves, resulting in better choices, improved self-regulation, and self-control.

Wise Decision Insight

Making a high-stakes decision typically consumes great energy, but following through with it often requires even more. Two elements must be considered:

1. The energy consumed in making the decision itself
2. The energy consumed in following through with the decision

Because so much is riding on the decisions we make throughout life, putting the decision-making process under a microscope with the intent of better understanding how wise decisions are made represents the central focus of this book.

Here is the reality of what we are up against in making wise, constructive decisions:

- Human beings are skillful **fiction-making machines**. Our brains are always working to get us what we want in life and can deploy a surprising number of ingenious reality-distorting strategies to do just that. If you want to buy a car that you really can't afford, eat unhealthy foods that you know are not good for you, or get involved in an office romance you know should never happen, be very careful because your brain can figure out a way to get you there. And the enabling distortion will happen without you knowing it!

  Yes, this marvelous neuro-processor between your ears is fully capable of getting you to the decision you want by twisting and biasing the information you are considering relative to the decision. In a real way, the human brain is fully capable of duping itself, of hijacking the decision-making process so completely that the only choice you have left is the one you actually wanted in the first place.

These reality-distorting mechanisms that your brain can unleash are not unfamiliar to the scientific community. They include motivated reasoning, confirmation bias, cognitive dissonance, rationalization, conformity dynamics, groupthink, and the boomerang effect to mention just a few.

To highlight and better appreciate the decision-making challenges we face because of the way our brains are wired, we only have to look at the first three just listed, namely motivated reasoning, confirmation bias, and cognitive dissonance.

- **Motivated reasoning** represents a nonconscious way of reasoning away contradictions that do not support the conclusions we want. Put another way, our own emotions are used to color the facts that are not aligned with our true desires and subvert the precise reasoning pathways that support wise and thoughtful choices. An example of this is line-calling in tennis. Players tend to see what they want to be true rather than what is actually true. In professional tennis, when a line judge calls a ball "out," players can be shocked by the call. Even when the call is confirmed by video replay, players argue that the technology must be off rather than acknowledging to themselves they were wrong.

- **Confirmation bias** is the tendency to unknowingly bias incoming information so that it supports our preexisting perceptions, beliefs, and desires. Sometimes referred to as "myside bias" or "self-fulfilling prophecy," confirmation bias is the insidious tendency to support and confirm what we already believe about something or someone in spite of evidence to the contrary. Confirmation bias has been shown to compromise decision-making in just about every arena of life, from politics to finance and from child rearing to personal health.

- **Cognitive dissonance** is the tendency to reduce tension and psychological distress arising from incoming contradictory information by nonconsciously altering the conflicting information so that the discomfort is reduced or completely eliminated. We resolve the dilemma by morphing, distorting, or altering the truth so we can sleep better at night and feel less conflicted, but at a very steep cost. In our brain's effort to get us what we want in life, it inadvertently undermines our most precious human asset, **our ability to make wise and sound decisions.**

- Wise decisions typically require balanced rational and emotional inputs. Short-term feelings of anger, fear, and anxiety can completely derail our decision-making process. Intense temporary emotions often lead to tunnel vision which blocks our ability to consider viable alternatives and options in our choices.

- Our moment-to-moment decisions can be heavily influenced by faulty mental and emotional learnings that were formed early in life. Wise decision-making can be seriously compromised by narcissism, poor moral character, little self-control, low self-esteem, poor stress management skills, and a harmful inner voice, often linked to early parenting practices over which the developing child had **no** control.

- We fail to **intentionally** establish clear criteria for granting or denying access to our decision-making command center. We fail to reality-test, to challenge our assumptions and beliefs with the potential consequence of allowing faulty data to flow directly into the core of our decision-making process.

- We unknowingly allow a voice to exist in our heads that has the potential to seriously undermine sound decisions. We'll call it your **inner voice.**

- We fail to upload sufficient decision-making **priorities** into our brain's command center that are critical for making wise, time-tested decisions (e.g. ultimate purpose for living, core values and beliefs).

- We fail to explore the full range of options that should be considered in the decision-making process. Tunnel vision can tragically restrict legitimate alternative choices.

- We underuse our brain's capacity for **reflective consciousness,** our ability to step outside ourselves, reflect on the reality of what's actually happening, and confront the potential consequences of the decisions we make.

Concrete strategies for dealing with all of these issues will be
detailed in the chapters that follow. It's important that you read this
book from two perspectives. The first is from the perspective of how
the information can improve your own decision-making skills, and the
second is how you can use the information to improve the decision-
making skills of others.

THE CASCADE OF POOR DECISION-MAKING

Here is an example of how so-called small, seemingly inconsequential
decisions can result in completely unanticipated negative outcomes.

- Poor Decision 1: You stayed up late drinking too much wine
  to soothe your nerves about a nerve-wracking and highly consequential presentation you're giving for major out-of-town
  corporate executives the next day, hoping that afterward they
  will offer you the massive job opportunity you've dreamed
  of and worked toward your whole life. Despite knowing that
  wine after dinner crushes your sleep quality, you opt for that
  extra glass. A brutal night of sleep is precisely what happens
  as a result. Like clockwork, you are up counting sheep at
  2:15 a.m., and you awake the next morning wondering if you
  slept at all, your brain running on fumes. Your body's hunger
  signals are totally malfunctioning too, as sleep deprivation
  throws the hunger hormone ghrelin (the one that messages
  your brain to stop eating when you are full) totally off kilter.
  Your brain is screaming *"I'm hungry; I need to eat now!"* as
  a result, despite having had steak and potatoes, broccoli and
  buttered bread, chocolate cake and ice cream, and wine just
  before going to bed.

- Poor Decision 2: You make your way to shower and get yourself dressed, all the while trying to clear the mental haze for
  the big day ahead, dimly aware of a gnawing sensation that
  you are *famished*. In a dreamlike state of a foggy mind and
  sluggish body, a spur-of-the-moment decision to skip your
  morning workout and make a pit stop at Dunkin' for some
  fast-acting sugar and caffeine somehow seems like an excellent

idea. *"I need some quick fuel to wake up, so I can be cogent and ON for the day ahead."*

- Poor Decision 3: You arrive at the office, the wave of glucose from breakfast rushing through your bloodstream. You are in a sugar-fueled high-energy state, alert and raring to go, if perhaps a little rushed and scattered. There's an hour to go before your presentation, which you were going to put the finishing touches on, but you get stuck on Googling homes in the neighborhood you'd like to move to with your family when you get the promotion. You are flying high, and it feels like a *when* and not an *if*! In checking out real estate sites, you neglect to check your inbox, which holds important information about your upcoming meeting.

- Poor Decision 4: You bookmark compelling web pages as you go, dreaming about what it's going to be like to live in your dream location and have your dream job. This fantasy is so enrapturing that time flies, and all of a sudden you have two minutes to get into the boardroom. The executive team is on site, and will be ushered into the boardroom right on time. You usually arrive at least 20 minutes before your presentations, to make sure technology is functioning properly. This time, your mind squarely planted in visions of the future, your sugar buzz just starting to wear off, you think to yourself, *"I'm sure it will be okay."*

- Poor Decision 5: You arrive in the boardroom and discover that the technology set up is *not* okay. Not even remotely! Curveball! *"Why did I not arrive early as I usually do? Why did I not exercise this morning to get fresh oxygen into my brain cells and reset my biochemistry? And why on earth did I have that last glass of wine that I knew would disrupt my sleep!?"*

- The technology team comes right away, but it's 20 minutes before it's all sorted and you can start your carefully polished presentation, one you've put months into developing so it's absolutely perfect. But between the late start, the now full-force sugar crash, and the mental fog hampering your capacity to respond thoughtfully and intentionally to complicated, nuanced questions posed by the executive team, and their complete and utter shock that the scenario is unfolding at all ("*Is **this** the person we were going to hire to lead the new strategic initiative??*"), the whole interaction goes pear-shaped. They look at one another in a knowing way, recognizing that they must continue the search until they find the right person.

Because of this sequence of events, you don't *get* the opportunity to have the conversation about moving your family to a new city for what had promised to be an exciting new chapter in everyone's life. All this occurred because you failed to make the right *small* decisions, which compromised your ability to shine in the crucial moments.

As we will learn in Chapter 1, it's hard, if not impossible, to make thoughtful, wise decisions when we fail to make our health and wellness high priorities.

Wise decision-making is an acquired competency that takes targeted, repeated investment of energy over time to achieve proficiency. And the neuroscience is clear, with consistent and diligent practice, the return on investment (ROI) is substantial. Changing the way we make decisions is hard work, but human transformation can and does happen when we set our sights on a goal and follow through with persistence and dedication.

Nothing short of the success of our lives, as well as the lives of the children we are so fortunate to influence on a daily basis, is at stake! The overarching goal of this book is to equip parents, teachers, coaches, and others with a concrete, science-based method for helping adults and youth achieve timeless wisdom in their everyday choices. As adults, we can be powerful decision-making examples for young people who see, emulate, and learn from the way we make choices.

In becoming lifelong students of wise decision-making ourselves, we not only demonstrate the multilevel value of being a forever learner, but simultaneously embed a priceless life skill in young people during their most malleable period of development across life. By demonstrating true wisdom in our own lives, we teach our children how to tap into their own decision-making superpower, something we will call their own personalized **Y.O.D.A.** And that is the gift of a *lifetime*.

PART I

YOUR OWN DECISION ADVISOR (Y.O.D.A) FUNDAMENTALS

CHAPTER 1

Health Ignites Wisdom in Decision-Making

How, when, and why are the best decisions made? What does "making a good decision" even mean? What are the key characteristics? And, as the title of this chapter suggests, in what way does our multidimensional health play a critical role in our ability to make wise decisions, a capacity that stems directly from something we'll call your personalized **Y.O.D.A.**? Y.O.D.A. stands for **Your Own Decision Advisor**.

The central theme of this chapter is that our holistic health—mental, physical, emotional, and spiritual—is the vital starting point for sound, thoughtful, and measured decision-making. The headline: We simply cannot take in, consider, and thoughtfully process multiple streams of relevant information, both tangible and intangible, when we are anxious, depressed, sleep deprived, sedentary, isolated, and self-medicating with wine and M&Ms!

An uneven mind-body state like any of these only narrows the aperture through which we can fully see and think through life decisions of all shapes and sizes. And when we're running on fumes, letting self-care slip to the bottom of the to-do list, and not integrating our highest values and beliefs into the recipe, our decision-making capacity is inherently limited. This limitation holds whether the issue at hand is small (like "What shall I have for breakfast?") or large (like "Is it worth the family upheaval to move to another city for a more prestigious and better-paying job?"). The scenario presented in the introduction can happen to any of us. Whether in romantic relationships with our partners, as parents to our children, as colleagues in the workplace, and as members of our communities, we are just plain more apt to drop the ball and show up as a shadow of our capabilities when we don't rank health and well-being as a top priority. Health is, plain and simple, the foundation for all else!

It is the so-called little decisions that often are the highest-impact levers to influence the big ones, those that can have massive implications for changing the trajectory of our lives. Our everyday micro decisions set the table for the macro decisions that we know full well have the potential to change everything. And, without question, both our micro and macro decisions will serve to powerfully shape our ultimate destinies.

The whole point of decision-making, at all levels, is to continually fine-tune and fortify the process so that our lives increasingly represent who we most want to be in life. Wise decision-making sets the stage for us to authentically and powerfully embody the way in which we show up in the world.

DECISION-MAKING

The technical definition of the word "decision" is "a conclusion or resolution reached after much consideration." But what exactly constitutes a *good* decision? What are the main characteristics, and how can we think about framing our process to feel a sense of confidence and competence in making decisions and judgments that may well alter the trajectory of our lives and the lives of those we care about for months, years, or lifetimes? How can we trust ourselves to bring our decision-making best, the entirety of our physical, emotional, mental, and spiritual wisdom, when the stakes are highest, when the storms of life are raging, when we are fully aware that we are *not* at our mental and emotional best?

Stay tuned! In the pages that follow, we will provide concrete, practical answers to all these questions.

First and foremost, it's important to know that decision-making is a *learned behavior*. "Nurture," our life experiences and the environments we are exposed to, shapes "nature," the expression of our genes, hormones, neurotransmitters, and biochemistry, all of which will be detailed later in Chapter 7. We humans are a 24/7, 365-days-a-year work in process, with the events in our outside lives shaping our molecular-level makeup on the inside and which, in turn, continually shapes how we look, feel, behave, and make decisions in life.

Wise Decision Insight: Our decision-making is powerfully shaped by observing how those around us make decisions, especially during childhood and adolescence. We learn what good and responsible decision-making looks like by absorbing how the key people in our lives make their decisions, particularly those people closest to us. We learn by observing the impact of their decisions over time on all concerned. We may reflect upon emotionally charged scenarios with key adults in our lives later down the chronological timeline, pondering whether we'd have made the same call if in their shoes. Simply put, one of the most important ways we formulate our understanding of smart and wise decisions is by witnessing the decisions others make, some of which go well and others that go poorly. We continually adapt our own decision-making style accordingly.

Your *decision* to acquire this book speaks to the fact that you might be interested in expanding your understanding of wise decision-making and exploring ways to improve your own. This all starts with an awareness of potential benefits, followed by the decision to purchase.

Reflect for a moment on *how*, *why*, and *under what circumstances* you typically make your best decisions. Consider also how well your history of decision-making has held up over the long game of your life. Improving how we approach and execute on the decision-making process is *hard work*. Consciously making a decision is step one, and following through with it, day after day, embedding a new way of thinking and deliberation into your decision-making repertoire is where the rubber really hits the road. But when this happens, in a disciplined and consistent manner, what once felt like awkward new behavior, something you were trying on for size, becomes the automatic path of least resistance.

As we will learn, when we can see outside of ourselves, rising above a tricky decision-making moment to pause, reflect, and identify what's really going on, it is nothing short of our decision-making superpower. Put simply, our capacity for making sound choices is embodied in the power to *consciously reflect* and then act, rather than *impulsively react*.

Both research and experience have confirmed that basic things like being rested and healthy, achieving mental and emotional balance, and the like can, in and of themselves, facilitate better decision-making. When we consistently engage in healthy, growth-oriented behaviors, such as conscientious self-care, we steadily begin making decisions that are more thoughtful, are wiser, and are more aligned with our most cherished values and long-term goals.

Our Brains and Bodies Are One Dynamic Integrated System

If there's one fact biological and social science has made crystal clear, it is that the human mind and body operate as a **dynamically integrated system**. That's right, the *very same molecules*, neurotransmitters, hormones, immune system markers, gene expression patterns, and other biochemicals that shape our physical wellness *also* powerfully shape our mental, emotional, and spiritual wellness and, more broadly, our overall sense of well-being and happiness—and, not surprisingly, the quality of the choices we make.

"We are feeling creatures that think, not thinking creatures that feel," in the words of famed neuroscientist Antonio Damasio. And the basic job of the mind-body system is to integrate data from our internal state of being, our feelings, with relevant input from the outside world experienced through our five "sensory portals" (sight, smell, hearing, taste, and touch), to facilitate better choices and strive for a *positive* balance within the mind-body system.

On the topic of internal balance, a term scientists call "homeostasis," it's important to note that there's much more to existence and human health than simply maintaining a steady neutral state at a cellular level. The true underlying human drive is to move us toward a decidedly *positive* energy state. While we have a basic inner biological drive to stay alive, to breathe, digest, and maintain on average a 97.8 degree temperature, our stronger intrinsic motivation is to *flourish*.

Accordingly, we can think of our integrated mind-body systems as continuously striving to achieve a net positive homeostatic state, driving energy throughout our brain and body in a manner that ups the odds for conscientious and responsible life choices.

Another important understanding is this: Conceptualizing health in discrete black-and-white categories of physical, emotional, mental, or spiritual capabilities is misguided and *overly simplistic*. The barebones fact is that health is highly nuanced, fluctuating with our biochemistry and lifestyle choices. Health is, by its very nature, a series of interactive, integrative molecular relationships, engaged in an ongoing, never-ending complex and sophisticated dance of nurture shaping nature, from the very start of life till the end. This fact represents a critical insight in our quest to make extraordinary decisions, as the chapters that follow will detail.

Scientific research is breaking new ground every day in terms of new and exciting discoveries about health and human potential. We know a fair amount about key mind-body dynamics and the neurobiological mechanisms by which they operate, but answering complicated questions and making big new discoveries most often simply leads to many more complicated questions. This is the beauty of evolution science, 3.8 billion years of the continuously unfolding story of cellular complexity, adaptivity, resilience, and growth.

Within this story of extraordinary scientific progress, a small handful of important molecules are known to powerfully sculpt our multidimensional health, and thereby our decision-making, and it is these which have received the preponderance of attention from researchers. The headline, after many decades of cutting-edge work, is that our health stems fundamentally from these under-the-skin molecular ingredients, ones that profoundly influence our growth and development through a dynamic biochemical cascade that flows throughout our entire integrated system. This all happens in a way even the most sophisticated researchers cannot pin down with absolute precision.

What's clear is that *everything affects everything else* and that changes can occur on a dime, consistent with our thoughts, behaviors, and life experiences. The vast majority of our knowledge about mind-body health comes from scientific research on the following biochemicals, the very same ones affecting the mind and the body in dynamic and interactive ways, which in concert play a role in how we approach, make, and follow through with our daily decisions. (See Figure 1.1 for a basic overview of how it works.)

- **Oxytocin:** The "love" neuropeptide (molecules that can cross the blood-brain barrier) is a key ingredient in the recipe for positive feelings stemming from human bonding and love.

- **Opioid-like neuropeptides:** Mother Nature's built-in pain relievers and the biological wellspring of euphoria, catalyzed by social connection and physical touch.

- **Serotonin:** Feel-good neurotransmitters that are natural happiness boosters and gastrointestinal system stabilizers.

- **Dopamine:** Mood-boosting neurotransmitters associated with novelty, excitement, and reward.

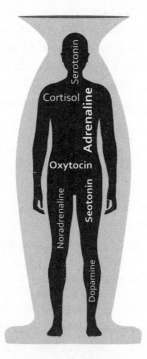

Figure 1.1   The human biochemical beaker.

- **Arginine Vasopressin:** Neuropeptides that regulate water, homeostasis (balance), and kidney function.

- **Cortisol:** Known as the "stress hormone," cortisol influences inflammation, blood sugar levels, metabolism, and memory formation. Social support helps to keep cortisol levels in equilibrium.

- **IL-6 and IL-8:** Immune system biochemicals, cytokines, that are involved in the inflammatory response in the case of acute injury (e.g. sprained ankle), chronic disease (e.g. type 2 diabetes), and autoimmune disorders (e.g. rheumatoid arthritis), as well as mental and emotional health conditions such as anxiety, depression, and other major psychiatric disorders. In short, the inflammatory effect of these molecules is systemwide, affecting the function of both the brain and the body.

As discussed throughout the chapter, our mind-body systems are integrated and dynamically changing, with the same molecules that affect one element of our health affecting others. And now that you have a sense for the most well-known beneath-the-skin molecules that influence our health, and how what influences one element of our health affects the others, let's delve more deeply into each discrete but interrelated dimension of health to further explore how health and decision-making are intimately connected at a cellular level.

PHYSICAL HEALTH AND DECISION-MAKING

Physical health is the easiest of all categories to understand. It's visible, tangible, and objectively measurable. Whether it's the common cold, a positive COVID test, a sprained ankle, a broken arm that needs a cast, or a blood test that's crossed the threshold for a low thyroid diagnosis, these are all things we can understand, tangibly see, quantify, and treat.

But deep inside of our bodies, in the depths of our viscera, our endocrine system, and the fluids where the biochemistry responsible for sustained life is predominant over all else, our brain is getting subtle and continuous bidirectional feedback via unique nervous system connections that powerfully and subconsciously shape the content of our minds and the choices we make. These intelligent, nonverbal bio-logic communication systems have evolved from the ground up, start-ing with our earliest ancestors here on planet earth. The information they provide, when made conscious, is nothing short of vital to both decision-making and survival.

Just as our experience of the outside world shapes our physical health (e.g., letting ourselves get run down, overdoing it, unhealthy eating, little or no movement or exercise), our inner molecular system is providing constant feedback through chemical signals designed to keep the whole system in homeostatic balance, a state of equilibrium the body constantly strives to return to, as mentioned earlier.

This means that while we may wake up with a headache, an achy back, creaky knees, or a runny nose, all which seem like "outside" issues affecting the physical body, there's a whole microscopic world of invis-ible processing and signaling happening deep inside the body that in fact gave rise to these outer-facing issues.

Such nonvisible processing and messaging can unknowingly and dramatically influence how we think and feel. Biochemical sig-nals stemming from lack of sleep or inadequate nutrition to the cells can exacerbate mental and emotional stress, fostering an inflamma-tory neurochemistry that can erode sound judgment. It's hard to think clearly, not to mention make *good, thoughtful decisions*, when our bodies feel lousy. And indeed, physical health is just the tip of the iceberg in a much more intriguing, colorful, and exciting integrated story.

EMOTIONAL HEALTH AND DECISION-MAKING

Lest you think of emotions as fuzzy, ephemeral, nonrelevant sensations that come and go on a whim, stay tuned, because here is what we know:

Emotions represent critical decision-making data.

Indeed, emotions can be just as important as fact-based infor-mation in making wise decisions, sometimes even more so. As a quick example, when one's gut feeling says no to a decision, perhaps there's something the conscious mind should be considering in the delibera-tive process.

As we will cover later in the book, emotions are distinct from feelings, but intimately related. How? *Emotions are subconscious* biochemical processes that underlie what we experience as *conscious feelings*. In other words, emotions and feelings are two sides of the very same coin. Our emotions, which have their own individualized biochemical signatures, initiate in both the viscera of the body and structures of the brain a specific molecular cocktail depending on the emotion evoked.

For example, your stomach feels tight as you think about giving an important presentation to the senior management team at your company. Your body is talking to you, expressing an emotion at a subconscious physiological level, which surfaces as the feeling of fear. And why fear? Whatever interpretation your mind has contrived regarding your presentation, it is perceived to be a threat. Put another way, our feelings and their underlying emotions simply reflect our perception of the world as we experience it. Depending on the meaning we give to any given situation, the result can be anger, joy, disgust, compassion, or hatred, and each feeling state will influence our decision-making process in a different way.

It is here that we can take concrete steps to protect our decision-making machinery by acknowledging and interpreting the feelings that are currently surfacing and by framing and reframing our perceptions of what's happening around us so that our emotional responses support sound decisions rather than against them. This understanding will be further explained in Chapter 12.

As with other areas of health, there is a continuum along which our emotions and feelings operate. In this case, while you may not be able to swing from one pole to the other (e.g. transforming massive anxiety into complete unbridled excitement), you *can* upshift your feelings to an area of greater upside with positive self-talk, like "I've done all I can to prepare, and yes I'm nervous, but I'll keep breathing, approach this as a learning experience, and see what unfolds." And by the way, this constructive inner dialogue can reduce stress and help clarify the alternatives you have before you.

Some individuals tend to be more emotionally vulnerable to the effects of their environments than others, an area of scientific study called "biological sensitivity to context." Those on the more sensitive side of the biological continuum are termed "orchids," while the heartier and more resistant individuals are called "dandelions." Have you noticed that some aren't bothered by traffic jams, discourteous drivers, or loud noises, while others decidedly are?

Everyone is wired differently from birth, and these differences are observable at the very start, as newborns lie in their cribs in the hospital, some more sensitive to light or noise than others. These differences in sensitivity are stable and persist throughout life. This means that some people are simply more biologically susceptible to mental and emotional stress and must work more diligently to manage inner chemistry than others—or their decision-making will suffer.

It's also important to understand that when our emotional chemistry is primarily generated by negative life events, over time the molecular cocktail of stress biochemicals, if not offset by positive emotion, can seriously compromise our health and good judgment. Just consider how feeling sustained low motivation and resentment can result in a kind of cognitive fog that fosters careless errors, impulsivity, and, most importantly, bad choices.

Wise Decision Insight: The choices we make can be profoundly influenced by our current emotional state via molecular processes residing deep below the surface and hidden from view, for better or worse. The solution: *Do everything possible to constructively alter a dysfunctional emotional state before making important decisions.*

Mental Health and Decision-Making

While the stigma regarding mental health is slowly waning, and rightfully so, we have a very long way to go as global citizens to establish programs and systems that support the prevention and treatment of mental health issues. From a scientific perspective, mental wellness should be prioritized and valued equally to taking our child to the pediatrician for a bacterial infection or sprained ankle, or being disciplined about making our own annual adult visit to the internist, if for no other reason than to set the stage for sound decision-making throughout life.

To reiterate, the very same chemicals that contribute to vibrant emotional health are the same ones that contribute to vibrant mental health, just further upstream. Well-managed mental health is a *significant* contributor to wise decision-making. Depression, panic disorders, chronic anxiety, and all forms of mental unwellness are simply signals that the mind-body system is out of balance and something needs to be adjusted to remediate the issue or the decision-making process can be seriously derailed. If decisions must be made while feeling mentally unwell, a brief bout of physical exercise, a walk outside in nature, an oxytocin-producing conversation with a wise and trusted friend, slow and deep breathing, a kindness meditation, and the like can add immeasurable short-term clarity in your effort to make the right choice.

Much of what we suffer from today—specifically anxiety and depression as the two largest categories of mental unwellness—is capable of completely sabotaging how we think about the choices we make. Understanding how basic things like getting adequate sleep, exercise, eating healthy food, practicing mindfulness, spending time in nature, and investing energy in high-quality relationships can be leveraged to elevate mental clarity and more grounded, reality-based thinking represents a critical *mental* decision-making insight.

Any strategy that gives rise to a more clear-headed, mentally focused, fully engaged sense of confidence and competence, even if only short term, should be given serious consideration. Anything that helps get one's mental thinking firmly on the solid ground, to mentally deal with, in the words of Shakespeare, life's "slings and arrows" *before critical decisions are made* must be considered.

In summary, what affects one biochemical element of our mind-body system inherently cascades through all the others and can take place in the blink of an eye or, in some cases, very slowly. What matters most is that when the right biochemical agents are released at the right time and in the right amount, the result is the ideal recipe for balanced, thoughtful decisions. And what's exciting in this understanding is that we can exert considerable influence over the timing and concentrations of those chemical ingredients with proper training and preparation. For example, realizing the importance of the decisions you will be making tomorrow, your inner voice (your Y.O.D.A.) might send the following coaching advice:

"No impulsive drive-through dinner for me tonight, I'll go home and prepare a healthy dinner and get a good night's sleep. On the new job decision, I'll ask for the time I need to think it through and get as much input as I can to clarify the risk-reward. I will make the decision when I am calm, rested, and mentally prepared."

SPIRITUAL HEALTH AND DECISION-MAKING

Now that we've covered three of the four mind-body dimensions of health, we're ready to cover the big one. This is the dimension of *spiritual health*, the major higher-order driver of who we are, what we stand for, and who we ultimately become.

All energy systems inherently gravitate toward *entropy*, defined as a gradual decline in order and organization, or conversely a slow descent into chaos and disorder. Spirituality, for reasons related to having a sense of belonging to something larger than oneself and a connection to other human beings, helps prevent individuals from feeling a sense of hopelessness and isolation. Research shows that isolation, being and feeling alone, is as harmful to one's health, by virtue of the very same molecules described earlier, as being obese or smoking 15 cigarettes per day.

Put simply, spiritual energy, which at its core is purpose, is the ordering force in the energy system of human existence. Having a clear sense of purpose, values, and beliefs organizes, coordinates, and streamlines human energy rather than allowing it to gravitate toward chaos and disorder.

While spirituality is often thought of as an individual's religious beliefs, it is technically defined as relating to or affecting the human spirit or soul as opposed to material things. It's interesting that spirituality has rarely been linked to the topic of overall health, both in everyday conversation and in scientific research. This understanding, however, is starting to change. What we now know is that spiritual experiences center our biochemistry via the very same mechanisms that drive our mental, physical, and emotional health.

Wise Decision Insight: The brain's processing of spiritually driven thoughts, ideas, and experiences gives rise to health-promoting biochemical ingredients in the mind-body system that are essential to wise and timeless decisions.

"When you are inspired by some great purpose, some extraordinary project, all your thoughts break their bounds. Your mind transcends limitations. Your consciousness expands in every direction."

—Yoga Sutras of Patanjali

In summary, human beings are complex, multidimensional energy systems. One's highest beliefs, purpose, values, and connection with others energize the brain and body in ways that promote health at a molecular level and, equally important, serve to align our decisions with our highest priorities in life. The spiritual dimension represents the ordering force in determining what matters most to us in life. As such, spiritual insights play a critical role in our ability to look back in time and say, "I'd make that same decision again today given the same circumstances." When that happens, we know we've made the right decision.

Wise Decision Insight: To ensure our most important decisions in life are fully aligned with our deepest values and purpose, our spiritual dimension, it's vital to spell out, in the clearest terms possible, what our core purpose, values, and beliefs are in order to properly equip our inner decision-making advisor (Y.O.D.A.) with the required navigational coordinates.

Y.O.D.A.

We can think of your Y.O.D.A. (Your Own Decision Advisor) as a set of metaphorical bumpers that keep your life decisions in the bowl-able part of the lane. There is some degree of flexibility on the trajectory of the ball, yet the bumpers provide protection from getting sidelined into the dead-end drain of the alley before even having a shot at knocking down any of the pins.

In other words, if the ultimate goal is a strike, where all 10 pins go down, and the worst-case scenario is a scratch, wouldn't you prefer to knock down even one or two, a decision that perpetuates momentum in the right direction? This provides an opportunity to bowl a spare, eliminating the rest of the pins on the second go-around, and is, by a wide margin, a lower-risk and higher-reward strategy.

Let's face it, hitting a perfect strike 100% of the time, in bowling or in life, is a low-odds bet. But aiming for gradual progress, fine-tuning your decision-making skills, is highly reasonable and rational. And in the end, wouldn't you prefer slow, steady progress, a few pins at a time, to being *out of the game* before even having the opportunity to score a point?

The objective of this chapter has been to provide clear insight into the vital link between physical, emotional, mental, and spiritual health and sound decision-making, with the goal of being able to actively and intentionally engage in building adaptive habits and behaviors that support your multidimensional health. (See Figure 1.2.)

Later chapters will outline the details for creating your Y.O.D.A. roadmap, complete with operating instructions and written exercises, all designed to most effectively and efficiently discern the elements of central importance to you, to keep you out of the alleys and in the lane, building and fortifying your physical, emotional, mental, and spiritual literacy muscles with every decision you make.

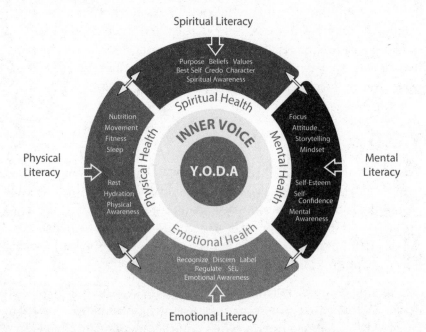

Figure 1.2   Health ignites wisdom in decision-making.

CHAPTER 2

Getting Through to the Inner Core

"I'm trying to get through to you but it's impossible."

"I know you hear what I'm saying but it's not getting through that thick head of yours!"

We all clearly have the ability to hear something being said but not let the message reach into the central core of where we reside. One way of referring to this special inner core might be the command from center of our brains. Through some yet-to-be-fully-understood series of mechanisms, incoming messages can be totally blocked and are DOA: dead on arrival. Alternatively, some can be partially blocked, such that we hear only what we want to hear, and others can be allowed inside fully intact, as is.

The point is that nearly everyone in our life wants access to our inner command center because that means they have the opportunity to influence the decisions we make. The innermost you is sought after by parents, teachers, coaches, religious leaders, politicians, employers, family members, TV advertisers, and on and on. Entry into your command center means the door to changing your thoughts, your behavior, and your choices is open.

Here are some examples of blocked messages:

- A father tries to convince his son not to use recreational drugs, but the son subconsciously blocks the messages from reaching his inner core. As the father is speaking, he realizes his words are having little or no impact on his son.

- A mother constantly tells her older children to attend church on Sunday. They hear her words, but the words are blocked from reaching their inner core.

- A wife continually conveys, verbally and nonverbally, that the lack of emotional safety she feels in the relationship is eroding her trust, and the marriage. Her message is dismissed and ignored.

- A couple agrees to a free trip in Las Vegas in return for attending a time-share sales class. Both hear the persuasive presentation but both prevent the information from penetrating their inner command center. They do not purchase a time-share unit.

- A high school teacher persistently sells her political ideology in her classes. Some students are able to completely prevent her political persuasions from entering their inner control center.

- A husband attempts to convince his wife that she needs to be more sympathetic and encouraging with their two boys in competitive sports. His message falls on deaf ears.

- A best friend tries to convince his buddy to exercise more regularly to lose weight. The friend is 100 pounds overweight. The heartfelt words go nowhere.

- It's time to buy a new car but upon arriving at the dealership, you are confronted by a very pushy, overly dramatic salesperson. You hear all of his words but nothing he says connects with you. You leave the dealership and vow never to return.

Here are some examples of being granted open access to someone's command center:

- For whatever reason, I fell hook, line, and sinker for everything she said. I ended up making some terrible choices.

- I instantly liked the salesperson at the dealership. I found myself really trusting almost everything he recommended. I ended up buying a car that was too expensive and the wrong color. I have deep buyer's remorse.

- I've always trusted my friend so when she encouraged me to try some drugs, I agreed. I have so many regrets about that first decision.

- Most of my friends find ways to cheat on tests. They convinced me to do the same and now I'm cheating too.

- I went on a week-long Outward Bound trip with my dad. For the first time in years, I started hearing what he was saying to me. I really was headed in the wrong direction.

- I get the same feedback from my colleagues at work every year. For some reason, this year's survey results really got to me. I'm sincerely trying to make changes.

- I love and trust my coach. I do everything he tells me without hesitation.

THE GATEKEEPER

Here are a couple of important questions: First, what is the connection between decision-making and one's command center and, second, what is the process by which access to our inner command center is granted or denied? The answer to the first question is that one's command center represents the location where decisions are actually made in the brain.

The answer to the second question is more complicated. Clearly there are some criteria, whether conscious or not, for determining which messages are let through and which are blocked. With that in mind, let me reintroduce you to **Y.O.D.A.** This is not the YODA of *Star Wars* but there are some similarities. As we learned in Chapter 1, this Y.O.D.A. stands for Your Own Decision Advisor.

Here are some wise decision insights:

- Y.O.D.A. is the senior resident in charge of our command center. We all possess a Y.O.D.A., but there are vast differences in effectiveness and good counsel.

- Y.O.D.A. represents our inner resident coach and master decision maker.

- Y.O.D.A. is an acquired competency that continues to evolve throughout life, a skill that can be intentionally built and strengthened, just like any other muscle.

- Y.O.D.A. can be a blessing or a curse, depending on the advice given.

- To be your best advisor possible, Y.O.D.A. should be preloaded with critical life coordinates such as core values, beliefs, and core purpose in life.

- The exact neurological location of Y.O.D.A. is still in question but the human insula appears to be a major contributor. (See Figure 2.1.) Hidden deep within the sulcus of the brain, the insula subserves a wide variety of functions, ranging from sensory and emotional processing to high-level cognition. The insula processes visceral sensations, autonomic reactions, somatic and auditory processing, decision-making, attention control, cognitive functions, and speech. Although neuroscience has not found a single place where decisions and self-awareness are located in the brain, the insula clearly plays a central role.

- Y.O.D.A. is highly trainable and is the primary target of this book. Your own resident advisor holds the keys to extraordinary decision-making.

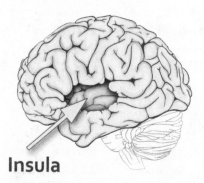

Insula

Figure 2.1 The insula.

THE BLOCKING AND TACKLING OF DECISION-MAKING

Whether you are blocking information from getting through to your brain's central command center (holding your defensive line) or are tackling a difficult decision and trying to get it right, the neuro-processor between your ears is receiving neural signals from multiple areas of your brain. (See Figure 2.2.)

The neurological footprint of every decision is different and entirely unique. Even your effort to block information from getting through to your inner core represents a decision, whether conscious or subconscious. Prior to every decision, neurons send coded messages through sudden bursts of electrical signals. We make decisions based on the cumulative sum of all related neurological inputs, both positive and negative. Most decisions, both blocking and tackling, are made quickly and subconsciously based on previously acquired habits.

So the big question is: Where did the acquired habits come from and how were they formed? Were they intentionally acquired and do

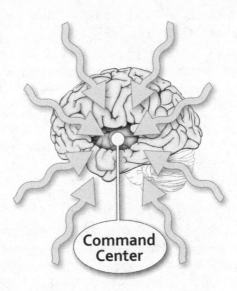

Figure 2.2   The command center.

they actually support responsible and wise choices? Most people report little understanding about how or when habits were formed, habits that play such a pivotal role in the day-to-day choices we make. An important objective of this book is to change that. Rather than allowing the process of habit formation to occur automatically without reflection, a consciously determined vetting process for decision-making will be detailed in Chapter 5. Once the vetting process guidelines are clearly established, the next step is to automate that process itself. Converting that process into a habit occurs with regular, intentional practice. Once habituated, all decision-making will automatically be screened through a predetermined set of lenses you put in place.

To better illustrate how the fine-tuning of the habit acquisition process occurs, let's use the example of shooting a basketball. The decision to take the right shot occurs in milliseconds, but the learning process occurs gradually over time. An important element of coaching basketball is teaching players good decision-making habits around shooting. Helping players learn when to take a shot and when not to represents an important aspect of successful coaching. When players first start playing, the decision to shoot is haphazard and undisciplined. Gradually, players begin learning what constitutes a good versus a bad shot-making decision. Considerations such as distance from the basket, the position of the defender, time remaining on the clock, the player's shot-making competency from different distances, and their mental and emotional state are intentionally and consciously used to improve shot-making decisions. With repeated practice and feedback from the coach, the entire process eventually becomes automatic and instinctive. Taking the right shot at the right time, regardless of whether it is successful, becomes an instantaneous decision requiring little or no conscious deliberation.

Some decision-making lends itself to being completely automated, occurring without conscious deliberation, while others do not. Things like shooting free-throws in basketball, eating healthy foods, exercising regularly, or always being 10 minutes early for appointments can, with training, be converted into habits. Other decisions, however, require measured consideration. Momentous decisions fall into this category. Examples might include: Should I get a divorce?

Should I have a complete shoulder replacement? Should I get a second vaccine booster shot? Should I put my daughter on anti-anxiety medication? Some decisions require days and even months of vetting to get to the right decision.

An interesting decision-making scenario is deciding what to order from a restaurant. Some people scan the menu and can decide very quickly, whereas others struggle to decide what to choose. They often wait for everyone to order and may even ask others what they think the best choice for them would be. If vetting habits around food selection have already been acquired, deciding what to order from the menu is vastly easier. Qualifiers might include considerations like low-fat, small portion size, dairy-free, vegan, gluten-free, and the like. Once the vetting process is acquired, making the right choice can occur nearly instantaneously.

Here are some wise decision insights:

- Every person possesses an inner core where decisions are processed. For the purposes of this book, this will be referred to as the central command center.

- The command center is capable of receiving a vast array of neurological signals from geographically dispersed regions of the brain in decision-making. Such inputs are critical in making sound decisions.

- Cutting-edge neuroscience suggests that the human insula plays a central role in the command center's operation.

- Everyone wants access to the inner core of a person, because that opens the door to influencing a person's choices.

- Human beings are capable of consciously or subconsciously granting or denying access to the command center of their brains.

- Some decisions are completely under the control of habit and require little or no deliberation. Others (such as which member of your family should be chosen to act as executor of your will) require thoughtful and careful consideration.

- Whether conscious or not, our brains are referencing something in granting or denying access to our command center as well as in making the right decision. An important objective of this book is equipping Y.O.D.A. with a consciously designed vetting process for both.

- Converting the vetting process to a well-established habit that automatically surfaces whenever important decisions are to be made represents the final step in ensuring better and more responsible decisions.

CHAPTER 3

The Voices in Our Head

When you speak from that deep, inner voice, you are really speaking from the unique tabernacle of your own presence. There is a voice within you that no one, not even you, has ever heard. Give yourself the opportunity of silence and begin to develop your listening in order to hear, deep within yourself, the music of your own spirit.

—*Anam Cara*, by John O'Donohue

There are some crucial points to understand. First, "voices in our head" are completely normal. We all have them. Second, getting through to your inner core, your central command center, means getting through to your *inner voice*, which represents the power broker in decision-making. Inner speech is the brain's way of talking to itself. One's inner voice, which only that person can hear, is the brain's gatekeeper, chief storyteller, and, most importantly, **master decision maker.** One's inner voice is direct talk from the brain's command center. Man's remarkable capacity for complex language has equipped the brain with the ability to speak to itself through words.

The younger the brain, the more sensitive and malleable to inputs from the outside world. The child's brain is a super-charged learning machine. Inputs to the infant brain come primarily from visual, auditory, and kinesthetic stimuli. Evidence suggests that auditory inputs and biological messages are transmitted even prenatally from the voices of parents, grandparents, siblings, and others, but most particularly the mother.

Termed "maternal-fetal synchrony," the mother and unborn child communicate in profoundly impactful ways throughout pregnancy, both verbally and nonverbally. The fetus absorbs all, and in addition to hearing their mother's voice and tone, any stress or discomfort that activates maternal cortisol passes through to the fetus as well, via cortisol receptors on the placenta. When the mother's heart rate or blood pressure go up, the fetus responds accordingly.

These inputs (multilevel messages) are stored in the more primitive areas of the fetal brain (brainstem and limbic system) because the higher-order brain (cortex and neocortex) is not yet adequately developed to have capacity to make sense of these messages. Importantly, maturation and integration of these higher-order brain structures is a process that unfolds through an individual's late 20s and early 30s.

As the child's capacity for language develops, the totality of sensory inputs eventually takes the form of a crude internal private narrative. This represents the beginning of one's inner voice, something we'll call Inner Voice 1. The message and the tone of this developing voice is a direct reflection of the accumulated neurological inputs from parents, teachers, siblings, and so on. Inner Voice 1 is formed and operates for the most part unconsciously. It flows directly from one's central command center. Characteristics of Inner Voice 1 include the following:

• Raw	• Untrained
• Uncensored	• Unpredictable
• Instinctive	• Impulsive/Reactive
• Unconscious	• Often embarrassing if made public

One's inner voice can be a significant detriment in life, or it can be a life-enhancing asset in our effort to make sound and responsible choices. It can, unfortunately, be overly self-critical, condescending, derogatory, caustic, immature, or narcissistic, anything but a wise advisor. It can also be supportive, encouraging, kind, insightful, patient, and wise. A dysfunctional voice breeds chaos and bad choices, and a healthy, constructive one breeds order and better choices.

It's important to understand that untrained Inner Voice 1 may or may not reflect the world as it actually exists. Distortions in what we see and the stories we tell ourselves are common. When the stories crafted by Inner Voice 1 are faulty or ill-conceived, the advice or decisions that emanate from those faulty interpretations will likely be flawed as well.

FROM INNER VOICE 1 TO INNER VOICE 2

Inner Voice 2 is the deliberate transformation of Inner Voice 1 into the voice of a great coach: reliable, mature, wise, and reasonable. Inner Voice 2 is intentionally acquired and consciously trained. Inner Voice 2 makes Inner Voice 1 conscious and unearths deficiencies and short-comings in tone and message. Inner Voice 2 can stop Inner Voice 1 instantly from going rogue. Inner Voice 2 is pre-coded with critical life navigational instructions (coordinates) that include:

• One's ultimate mission in life	• One's Best Self
• One's core purpose for living	• One's life scorecard of
• One's core beliefs	highest value
• One's core values	• One's personal credo

Inner Voice 2 is made possible from the evolutionary upgrade of conscious awareness. Humans are capable of being fully aware of the tone and content of their private, inner voice. The goal is to trans-form Inner Voice 1 into a masterful, reality-based resource filled with wisdom and great counsel that can be accessed throughout one's life.

Properly trained, Inner Voice 2 becomes a repository of wisdom, sound judgment, and perspective. It becomes the voice of a valued and trusted personal coach, one's own brilliant Y.O.D.A.

"YOU TALK" AND "I TALK"

The brain can coach and advise itself in the same way a coach talks, in the second person. We'll call it "You Talk": "You need to work harder." "You need to be more positive with yourself." "You have much more ability than you think."

Word messages in the first person we'll call "I Talk": "I should not be late." "I need to try harder." "I can do this." Both "You Talk" and "I Talk" can be helpful or destructive, wise or foolish. Both "You Talk" and "I Talk" can also be made public or kept entirely private. (See Figure 3.1.)

Just as we all have an acquired, untrained inner voice, we also have an acquired, untrained public voice; we'll call it Public Voice 1. Public Voice 1 is the brain speaking to itself publicly and, because it is raw, uncensored, and untrained, the tone and message may be shocking and completely inappropriate.

Trained public "You Talk," referred to as Public Voice 2, is "you" coaching "you," *out loud* with great wisdom and perspective. "You need to do this." "You cannot give up." You're saying such things out loud to yourself in your best trained public voice.

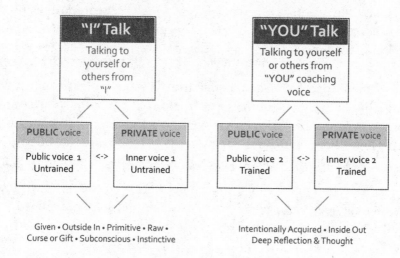

Figure 3.1 The voices in our head.

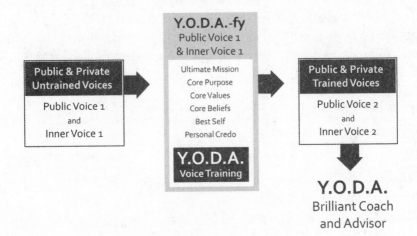

Figure 3.2   Transformation of Y.O.D.A.

An important focus of this book will be transforming Inner Voice 1 into Inner Voice 2: a wise and trusted advisor in making crucial decisions throughout your lifetime. The goal is to develop your own trained, brilliant resident advisor. (See Figure 3.2.)

CHAPTER 4

Time for Serious Reflection

Being aware of being aware of being. In other words, if I only know that I am but also know it, then I belong to the human species.

—Vladimir Nabokov

Now that you are more knowledgeable about the voices in your head, about where they came from, and about the critical role they play in the choices and decisions you make in life, let's turn the spotlight on your own private inner voice. Everyone possesses both a public and a private voice, but your private voice is closest to your inner core, your brain's central command center.

As Ethan Kross says in his excellent book *Chatter,* the inner voice is a basic feature of the human mind. Because one's inner voice plays such a critical role in decision-making and sound judgment, the questions that follow will focus mainly on your private rather than your public voice. Turn your attention inward and respond to the following questions as thoughtfully and honestly as possible.

1. At approximately what age did you become aware that you have a private inner voice?

    _____

2. What is typically the tone and content of your inner voice?

1	2	3	4	5
Decidedly Negative & Destructive				Decidedly Positive & Constructive

39

3. Would you be embarrassed or ashamed if your inner voice were made public?

1	2	3	4	5
Completely Ashamed & Embarrassed				Completely Okay with It

4. What has been the trajectory of your inner voice over the past two years?

1	2	3	4	5
More Negative & Critical				More Positive & Helpful

5. How much trust and confidence do you have in Your Own Decision Advisor (Y.O.D.A.)?

1	2	3	4	5
Little				Great

6. To what extent do you consider your personal Y.O.D.A. a great asset in decision-making?

1	2	3	4	5
Little				Great

7. To what extent have you considered your inner voice to be your life coach?

1	2	3	4	5
Never				Always

8. The tone and content of your private inner voice most reflects which of the following people in your life?

- Mother
- Father

- Grandparent
- Friend
- Coach
- Sibling
- Teacher
- None of the above

9. Is your private inner voice helpful or harmful as a general rule when you are under stress?

1	2	3	4	5
Mostly Harmful				Mostly Helpful

10. How much control do you have over how your private inner voice advises or coaches you?

1	2	3	4	5
Little Control				Considerable Control

11. To what extent do you feel the messages delivered by your private inner voice make a positive difference in your life?

1	2	3	4	5
Little Difference			Great Difference	

12. Rate the overall tone and content of your inner voice.

1	2	3	4	5
Too Harsh & Critical		About Right		Too Easy & Permissive

13. To what extent do you consider your inner voice a valued source of wisdom and perspective?

1	2	3	4	5
Not at All				Definitely

14. To what extent does your inner voice reflect your Best Self (the best version of yourself)?

1	2	3	4	5
Rarely				Often

15. To what extent does your inner voice provide the same kind of advice you'd give to someone you love who is facing a major decision point in their life?

1	2	3	4	5
Rarely				Often

16. Write a summary of the general tone and message of your inner voice when you are under stress, when you make mistakes, or when you face tough decisions.

_____

_____

_____

_____

17. Give one specific recent example of how and what your inner voice said to you when you faced a challenging moment.

_____

_____

_____

_____

BLOCKING OR GRANTING ACCESS

Just as a smartphone can be set up to block incoming calls or messages, so you can set up your Y.O.D.A. to prevent unwanted data from reaching you.

Here are some questions to ponder:

- Who do you allow unrestricted access to your inner core, to your Y.O.D.A. command center?

- Why them?

- Who are you constantly blocking? Is it intentional or does it just seem to happen automatically?

- Do you grant access to some who clearly should not be allowed in? Who are they and why have you granted them access?

- What criterion are you using for blocking or granting access to your inner core?

- What criterion *should* you be using for blocking or granting access?

Big Questions

What do you reference when you need to make an important decision in your life? Try to articulate your decision-making process and try to clarify the things you are likely to consider in making your decision. Put another way, where do you go for answers, for wisdom, and for great self-coaching?

Thoughts about this issue:

_____

_____

_____

_____

More reflections: are any of these true for you?

- I can rip on myself with no apparent repercussions, so I do.

- I take my frustration and anger out by attacking myself with vicious and demeaning words.

- Who better to dole out punishment than me on myself? Better for just me to see my inner struggles than the embarrassment of someone else looking on.

- I'm much more tolerant of others than I am with myself, and my inner voice is the evidence.

- I believe that if I punish myself with hurtful words, I will be less likely to do it again.

- I feel okay beating "me" up with my inner voice.

- Would you ever want someone you deeply care about to have your inner voice in his or her head?

- Sometimes I talk to myself out loud, making my private voice public, and I can be really shocked by what I say.

- I have little control over what I say to myself privately.

- Sometimes I feel scatterbrained from the constant chatter inside my head.

- Do the messages sent by your inner voice ever bring you inner peace and comfort in difficult and demanding times?

- I deserve the punishment because deep down I know I'm not worthy, maybe not even lovable.

- Who *is* that person inside my head? I wish they'd go away!

CONSCIOUS AWARENESS IS THE FIRST STEP

Transforming Y.O.D.A. into a trusted inner coach begins by reflecting on the issues and questions presented in this chapter. Because your inner voice is the voice of Y.O.D.A. and because it denies or grants access to your command center, it is imperative that the language and content of your inner voice be thoroughly examined and brought into the full light of reflective consciousness. Only when illuminated by this light, with as close to a 360-degree view as possible, can the issue be meaningfully and thoughtfully processed in order to make a solid decision.

Note: "Conscious awareness" and "reflective consciousness" will be used interchangeably throughout this book. Both refer to the brain's capacity to observe itself.

ASSIGNMENT

For the next five days, keep a written journal of the tone and content of your inner voice. At the end of each day, write a summary of what you learned regarding how you speak to and coach yourself. Write at least three sentences about what you discovered and any surprises or insights that surfaced.

CHAPTER 5

Equipping Y.O.D.A. with the Right Stuff

You've been dating someone for nearly six months now and as the weeks pass, something about the relationship is putting doubts in your mind that are quite disturbing. You fell deeply in love almost from the very first moment and quickly started thinking this was the person you wanted to spend the rest of your life with. But now you are not so sure. Questions about his honesty, fidelity, and capacity to truly love another person keep surfacing.

He seems increasingly preoccupied with his own needs and less about yours. You are pretty certain he is about to propose marriage. You are uncertain about what you should say or do. And this is precisely where a properly trained Y.O.D.A. can be of immeasurable value.

Here are just a few more examples:

- You witnessed a person run a red light and end up in a terrible collision. There were several major injuries. You don't want to get involved but you feel you should report what you saw.

- You caught your best friend in a bald-faced lie that was very hurtful to you. How should you handle it?

- Your boss asks you to do something clearly unethical. If you don't comply, you might lose your job.

- You've gotten yourself in the middle of a personal war on social media. You're not sure what to do or how to respond.

- Your husband wants your family to stay at your in-laws' home for the holidays. You cannot stand them. How should you deal with this?

- Your father is beyond difficult. You do not know how to manage him. What's the answer?

- You never get to do what you want to do. You always give in to what others want. You're not sure what to do about it.

- Your wife engaged in an unethical act that your daughter would be horrified to know about. You are afraid to confront your wife for fear of the anger it would produce and your concern it would fall on deaf ears.

- Your daughter constantly lies to you, so much so that it's hard to know what's real and what's not. You are her parent and love her unconditionally, but are concerned about this pattern manifesting later in life when the consequences will be vastly greater. How can you approach this in a way that doesn't feel threatening and attacking?

- Your son was accused of bullying other kids on the playground, and this is the second time it has happened. You are furious but yet not clear on how to handle it.

- A relative stole from you. You want to press charges but you're not sure it is the right thing to do.

- Your 22-year-old daughter has no desire to leave your home, and you don't think it is in her long-term best interests, to stay. You're uncertain about how to best approach the issue.

- You are in an abusive relationship that can flare up at any time. You're concerned about protecting yourself and your children. Your main concern is that they might come to believe that the damaging behavior is normal, repeating it in their own lives as grown-ups. What decisions should you consider now?

These and countless other examples call for wise, thoughtful, and measured responses. This is what Y.O.D.A. is all about, provided it is properly trained and equipped. Equipping, strengthening, and fortifying Y.O.D.A. is the central focus of this chapter.

PRELOADING Y.O.D.A. WITH THE RIGHT INFORMATION

Success in life is clearly about making the right decisions. A single bad decision can alter the trajectory of one's life in tragic ways for years. Human decision-making is a complex process that is influenced by our history, our life experiences, our moment-to-moment feelings and emotions, our needs and wants, our core values and beliefs, our understanding of the facts involved, and the strengths of our moral and ethical character.

Wisdom in decision-making represents an acquired capacity to grasp the deeper meanings of life, to prioritize what matters most in making life-altering decisions and choices. Being wise requires more than intelligence, superior knowledge, rationality, emotional intelligence, superior gut instinct, or simple goodness or kindness. It is also more than the dynamic interplay between personal reflection and an openness to experience.

Wisdom is the acquired ability to *rise above* the immediate demands and stresses of the moment; to make decisions that are grounded in transcendent values, core beliefs, and high ethical standards; and to achieve real and enduring perspective on the issues in question.

For Y.O.D.A. to coach us with time-tested wisdom, it must tap into our most noble side, referred to in Chapter 1 as our spiritual dimension. It is here that our core values, our sense of purpose and meaning in life, and our highest moral and ethical character reside.

EQUIPPING Y.O.D.A. WITH TIMELESS WISDOM

Your odds for summoning the wisdom of Y.O.D.A. are vastly increased when, as you have already learned, you are coming from a place of balanced mental, emotional, physical, and spiritual health.

The Vetting Process

The decision-making process can be greatly improved when viewed through seven lenses. Each of the lenses represents a distinct but related reference point for making the best and right decision:

1. Best Self

2. Best Moral Self

3. Life Purpose

4. Tombstone Legacy

5. Core Values and Beliefs

6. Personal Credo

7. Ultimate Mission in Life

The seven lenses are all interrelated, so it is to be expected that there will be some overlap in the vetting process. The ultimate objective is eventually to make this vetting process nearly second nature. One or more of the seven lenses will become your preferred Y.O.D.A. reference guide, and the scientific principle of neuroplasticity dictates that the more you practice, the more your Y.O.D.A. will begin to automatically materialize whenever you are facing important life decisions.

Before starting the seven lens process, the following questions should be considered:

1. What are the indisputable facts surrounding the decision? Put them down in writing.

2. What does your heart say is the right decision? How does your empathic self feel about what making this judgment call will mean?

3. What does your gut say is the right decision? Your gut response is the instinctive and automatic physiological feeling that points you in a particular emotional direction relative to a decision or situation. When you listen to your body, what is it telling you about the decision?

The Seven Lens Process

Lens 1:   Best Self

Write down the words that describe you at your absolute best, particularly when you are under stress or pressure. This is not a fantasy exercise. This is the actual you when you are most proud of yourself. Make a tentative decision for the dilemma you are facing through the lens of your "Best Self."

Lens 2:   Best Moral Self

From the following words, select the eight that best describe you at your moral and ethical best, when you are the proudest of your treatment of others.

Integrity	Humble	Authentic
Patient	Grateful	Compassionate
Kind	Generous	Loving/Caring
Honest	Empathic	Engaged

Make a tentative decision for the dilemma you are facing through the lens of your eight chosen words.

Lens 3:   Life Purpose

One's core purpose for living is the centerpiece of everyone's life story. Put your main reason for living down in writing.

_____

_____

_____

_____

Make a tentative decision for the dilemma you are facing through the lens of your core "Life Purpose."

Lens 4:   Tombstone Legacy

You get to select six words that will be carved into your tombstone. The words should reflect how you most want to be remembered after you are gone.

_____

_____

_____

_____

After you've selected all six words, make a tentative decision for the dilemma you are facing through the lens of your "Tombstone Legacy."

Lens 5:   Core Values and Beliefs

Write down your two most important values in life and the two most important beliefs you hold about life.

_____

_____

_____

_____

After writing them down, make a tentative decision for the dilemma you are facing through the lens of your "Core Values and Beliefs."

Lens 6:   Personal Credo

Your personal credo represents the current, most accurate articulation of what matters most to you in life. It is your internalized roadmap for a truly successful life. Your personal credo represents the scorecard of highest value to you.

_____

_____

_____

_____

After writing your personal credo and reflecting on it, make a tentative decision for the dilemma you are facing through the lens of your "Personal Credo."

Lens 7:   Ultimate Mission

Your ultimate mission is the one you must complete to qualify as having lived what you consider a truly successful life. This is the life mission for which failure is not an option.

_____

_____

_____

_____

Put into writing what you consider to be your ultimate mission in life and make a tentative decision for the dilemma you are facing through this lens.

It is important to understand that not all seven lenses will necessarily connect directly to the decision you are making. Simply take the insights gained from the seven lens process and make your final decision. If time permits, wait 24 hours before acting on your decision to be sure it still seems right.

An Important Note

The first seven lens process you undertake will require considerable time and energy for concentrated, high-quality reflection. For Y.O.D.A. to deliver wisdom in your decision-making and to advise you in a way that reflects thoughtful and measured perspective, all seven documents must be readily available mentally and emotionally for reference. The more you write about them, think about them, and rehearse them, the more available they will be to your resident advisor, your Y.O.D.A.

"The highest form of wisdom is kindness."

—The Talmud

CHAPTER 6

Protecting Your Inner Core at All Costs

Our brain exists fundamentally to help us survive and get us what we need and want in life. It is always listening for instructions. Since our inner voice is closest to our command center, the messages and instructions sent by our private voice will likely have the greatest opportunity for impact on the decisions we make. Our inner voice (IV) is analogous to an intravenous (IV) drip directly into the brain.

Advice and instructions are typically sent via words. Words, the meanings they represent, and the frequency of use create a narrative, one that goes *from* ourselves *to* ourselves. Every message creates a unique bioelectrical impulse, and repeated messages get the most neurological traction. This happens because a substance called myelin, a fatty sheath that insulates pathways in the brain, coats the most frequently used neural connections so that the electrical impulses can pass more easily and efficiently.

The brain assumes that frequently repeated messages are central to what we really need and want and to our survival, so it doubles down on making sure those messages get through as quickly and seamlessly as possible. If the same message keeps reappearing, the brain assumes *it must be important.*

So here is the critical question: How do we prevent false, biased, deceptive, contaminated data, and half-truths, distorted facts, outright lies, and falsehoods of all kinds from getting access to our control center and co-opting our decision-making process? In other words, how do we grow and strengthen our gatekeeping skills?

The reason this issue is so important is that once faulty or defective data gains access to our inner core, our ability to make sound judgments and good decisions will likely be compromised, with the result being that Y.O.D.A. cannot be fully trusted. (See Figure 6.1.)

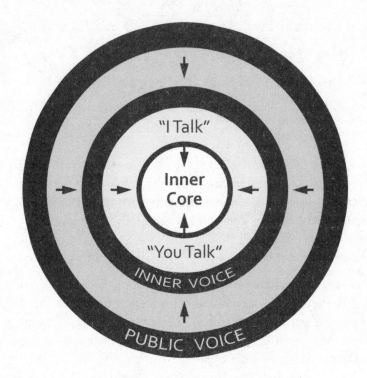

- Our Inner Voice is the gatekeeper to the Inner Core of the person (the Command Center).

- Our Inner Voice is the brain speaking to itself and is analogous to an intravenous drip directly into the brain.

- Y.O.D.A., equipped with the right operating instructions, facilitates gatekeeping decisions.

Figure 6.1   Gatekeeper to the inner core.

TAKING CHARGE OF YOUR INNER VOICE

Protecting Y.O.D.A. means controlling the flow of information that gets through to the command center of the person. There are four primary *controllable* sources of informational input:

1. Inner Voice Inputs

2. Public Voice Inputs

3. Visual Inputs: what you read and watch on screens

4. Auditory Inputs: what you hear and listen to

The vital fact is that you can exert *considerable influence* over all of these sources of input. You can consciously control what you say to yourself and the tone in which you say it. You can also control what you say publicly, what you read or watch, and what you listen to.

Humans have the capacity to immediately block some incoming messages, and others are only allowed access after careful scrutiny. The rapid, rigid, automatic blocking of information into our command center is called **Stage 1** control, and conscious discernment prior to entry is called **Stage 2** control.

It is in Stage 2 that the information can still be analyzed, fact-checked, and carefully scrutinized before full access is granted or denied. Stage 1 and Stage 2 control are essentially regulated by our inner voice, and the more skillful our inner voice is in opening and closing the gates at the appropriate times, the better prepared Y.O.D.A. can be in making wise and thoughtful decisions.

Television advertisers employ highly ingenious strategies to get viewers to lower their resistance to whatever is being sold. In other words, they aim to erode a person's Stage 2 control. Instinctively fast-forwarding through a TV commercial is Stage 1 control, and consciously setting aside new incoming information so it can be further analyzed is Stage 2 control. Famous celebrities are paid to endorse a product or service, a relaxing and soothing nature scene is portrayed in the background, inspirational music plays, well-known actors and actresses exude great joy and happiness—all of this is designed to get you to suspend your skepticism and open the gate to your command center.

All sales programs, no matter their shape or size, employ a specific and targeted strategy to override the inner gatekeeper's capacity to be discerning. The goal is to remove any and all obstacles to completing the sales transaction by gaining access to the inner you. Call it salesmanship, mind control, or subtle coercion, the key is always gaining access to the central core of the person. And since one's inner voice emanates directly from the command center of the person, it is the inner voice itself that holds the keys to the kingdom.

Because our inner voice most closely represents how we really think and feel about someone or something, it's as close to the real person as is humanly possible. Controlling an individual's public speech is but one important step in gaining control of the ultimate prize: our inner speech.

Understanding Resistance

Resistance is the refusal to adopt or accept something as true. Simply because we say something publicly does not mean that we actually believe it to be true. It also may not reflect how we actually feel on the inside. It's much easier to conceal our inner voice than it is our public voice.

When our public and private voices are fully aligned, the result is sincerity and authenticity. However, when our public and private voices are aligned with a potentially tragic decision, the deal is basically done. Our capacity for critical thinking and independent thought in that area is all but lost. To be clear, resistance is waged successfully or unsuccessfully at the level of our inner voice. Protecting our core from faulty data represents one of the most important battles we face as human beings. Connecting to the world in the way it actually exists demands we fight and win the battle for truth every day.

Truth Traps

- Because it feels true, it must be true.
- Because my closest, most respected friends believe it to be true, it must be so.
- Because I make a better impression when I believe it to be true (e.g. "I appear to be more intelligent"), I automatically tend to adopt it.

- Because she is better informed, better educated, smarter than I am, I accept her position as true.

- Because I know my weaknesses better than most, I can trust my version of reality.

- Because I'm fully aware of how people change their reasoning as their motivation changes, that's not going to happen to me.

- I'm 100% certain I've got the truth on this one.

- Because I never catch myself relying on rationalization to get what I want, I don't have to worry about this happening to me.

- Because I'm happier when I deceive myself (e.g. "It wasn't my fault"), I'm sometimes okay with it.

- When others challenge a core belief of mine, I feel justified in getting defensive and argumentative.

- Because some of my beliefs have become part of my core identity, I feel okay responding with righteous indignation when others attack those beliefs.

- *Objective* truth is in the eye of the beholder.

When we suspect incoming data is biased, deceptive, tainted, or corrupted, we must protect our Y.O.D.A. from being infected at all costs. And the greatest weapon we have in our defense arsenal is *conscious awareness*. The more we are consciously aware of the methods being used by others to control our thoughts and behavior, the greater resistance we can mobilize within ourselves to contain it.

More Insights About How Our Brain Works

The more we think a thought, regardless of its grounding in truth, the easier it is to access and the more real it is to us. In other words, it becomes our own personalized objective truth.

Debunking a bogus fact requires considerably more energy than accepting it as true. Conserving energy is a powerful influencer in our fight for fact-based truth. Mental laziness leads to laziness in interpreting the truth. When we hear others repeatedly embracing a belief, whether faulty or not, we are more inclined to accept it as true. And, unfortunately, when our gut tells us something is true, we're less likely to challenge its veracity. However, research has repeatedly shown that our gut can be completely wrong! Visceral feelings and emotions are intuitively based and do not necessarily represent the whole truth and nothing but the truth. They may represent the reality of how you feel but may not in fact represent the world as it actually exists. Just because a juror instinctively or intuitively feels a defendant is guilty in no way should be considered a measure of that defendant's guilt.

Here are some additional challenges we all face (including those listed in the introduction):

- We tend to reject contradictory evidence when it challenges a long-standing belief, particularly a core belief.

- Evidence that does not support what we now believe is often dismissed as faulty, biased, and inaccurate. Contradictory evidence that challenges a long-standing belief will likely not be investigated.

- We seek out people who share our beliefs and biases, and avoid people or discussions that challenge them.

- When we invest much of our identity in a core belief, whether grounded in reality or not, challenges to that belief are likely to be deeply disturbing and, therefore, vigorously defended.

- When a belief is consistent with what we deeply want or need, we are less likely to scrutinize its authenticity.

Human beings are fiction writers. Our brains are superb at concocting stories that allow us to do what we want and not feel badly about ourselves. To reiterate, we are *not* first and foremost rational creatures but rather emotional creatures who have the capacity to be rational. Our emotions run the show in life, and our capacity for logical thinking serves to moderate the flow of emotion. Every thought produces an emotion within milliseconds. Meaning and purpose in life come from the union of emotion and rational thought. Life without emotion would be colorless and empty. Life without rational thought would leave us completely at the mercy of moment-to-moment inner emotions and their accompanying outward-facing feelings.

GUIDELINES FOR PROTECTING YOUR INNER CORE

1. Assume most incoming data is partially or completely biased in some direction, whether intentionally or unintentionally (Stage 2 control).

2. Keep your incoming data protection system activated at all times (Stage 1 and Stage 2 control).

3. Quarantine all incoming data that poses a genuine risk of being contaminated until it can be properly vetted (Stage 2 control).

4. Become skillful at separating facts from opinions, both written and spoken (Stage 2 control).

5. Recognize when facts are selectively used to form a narrative that supports a particular bias. In your pursuit of the truth, make sure all the available facts are properly represented (Stage 2 control).

Wise Decision Insight

Sound and responsible decision-making requires that **Stage 1** and **Stage 2** control be activated at all times.

CHAPTER 7

Nature via Nurture: The Science of Uploading Y.O.D.A

Between stimulus and response there is a space. In that space is our power to choose our response. In our response lies our growth and our freedom.
—Viktor Frankl

Remember the "nature versus nurture debate"? The engaging and ever-popular cocktail party question about whether we humans are shaped more by our genes or by the environments we are in? Well, for the record, that debate is now a fully debunked urban legend of brain science, something called a *neuromyth*. Whether nature or nurture is more important in shaping who we become is, quite simply, the wrong question to ask. If you remember one thing from this chapter, it should be this:

We're shaped by both **nature and nurture**. Far from determining anyone's destiny, genes are merely a **starting point** for what's possible. The rest is up to us.

Our experiences in life shape our DNA and biochemistry in a dynamic and continuous symphony that unfolds across every age and stage in life. Our genes, inherited from our parents, can be thought of as the biological templates that instill *basic propensities* for who we become as human beings.

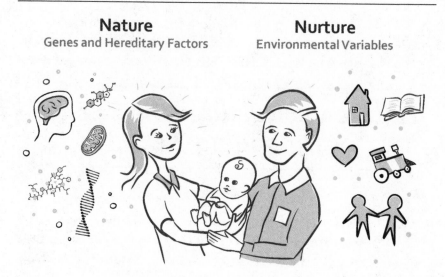

Figure 7.1 Nature and nurture.

Our experience of the world around us, from the moment of conception until we take our last breath, activates the expression of our genes on the inside in a way that shapes how we look, feel, and behave on the outside. Aside from a few rare single-gene traits (e.g. brown eyes) and diseases (e.g. Huntington's disease), the human characteristics that give rise to our stories and directly connect to issues of multi-dimensional health, personality, temperament, emotional intelligence, cognitive abilities, and decision-making are sculpted by thousands of genes activated by our life experience, in a way even the most sophisticated scientists can't pull apart.

Bottom line, our genes *do not determine* our fate in life. *We do.* And here's why.

Human beings have the unique capability for reflective consciousness, which embeds in each of us the capacity for self-determination and choice. Unlike our mammalian cousins, whose lives are primarily consumed by securing food, shelter, and survival, the higher-order networks in our human brains are capable of posing complex questions like "What is the purpose of my life?"; "What matters most to me?"; and "What's the right thing to do here?"

As we attempt to answer questions such as these, our brains are updating and constantly rewiring based on our responses and experience, a concept known as "neuroplasticity." This extraordinary neural malleability of the human brain represents a dynamic and iterative process that is unfolding every waking and sleeping moment across life. This unique capability enables us to make decisions based on what we've learned from the past, on what we project will be the future outcome, on whether the decision is aligned with our core values, and on what the actual odds are for success. We learn by experience, update our web of knowledge, then apply it to the future. It's our uniquely human ability to consciously reflect on our past experience and then intentionally choose a new course forward that opens the door to self-determined decision-making.

Here are three basic ways in which the outside world influences gene expression.

First, there are the *controllable* activities we choose and plan for, which shape our biochemistry simply by being in a predictable context, either solo or interacting with others. Some examples:

- You typically start your day with a 20-minute meditation followed by a workout to get your body up and ready for the day ahead. Today you set your alarm for 6 a.m., caffeinate and meditate, head out for a run by 6:30, promptly showering upon return so you can be ready to leave for work by 8 a.m. as you have an important 8:30 meeting, and you want to knock the ball out of the park!

- It's a 20-minute drive to get to your yoga studio, and your class starts at 9. You've organized your morning to get the children to school then run a few errands, leaving enough time to get to your class 10 minutes early so that you can lay out your mat and breathe in stillness before class starts.

- To balance out a very demanding and challenging week, you schedule dinner with a dear soul mate at one of your favorite restaurants to treat yourself. Just *thinking* about the dinner is transportive, instantly making you feel more relaxed and elevating your mood.

Second, there are the *uncontrollable and unpredictable* things that happen to us every day. Some are for the better, promoting biochemistry and gene expression patterns that boost health, energy, productivity, and happiness. A few positive examples:

- A wholehearted "I love you" from a beloved family member or friend brings joy.

- Your boss celebrates you at work for a job well done.

- A total stranger performs a random act of kindness.

But real life doesn't always work that way. Some percentage of random life experiences inherently fall into the "for worse" category, experiences that further exacerbate the downside if we're feeling mentally, emotionally, physically, or spiritually off-center—especially if we have no strategy to ground ourselves and proactively manage the situation.

These can trigger the release of stress biochemicals and inflammation-producing gene expression patterns, which over time can affect our mind and body in ways that are potentially harmful to us. For example:

- The beginning part of your morning routine goes to plan. But your computer crashes minutes before your 8:30 a.m. meeting and you have no backup copy of the presentation.

- Just before leaving the house, rushing to get out the door so all needed things can get done before your restorative yoga class, an innocent conversation with your spouse ignites an emotional landmine.

- You get into your car after a thoroughly exhausting day at the office to meet your friend for an evening that has been a mental oasis of joy all day long. The ignition in your car won't turn over. The engine light is on and you don't know why.

"ARGH!" you might say to yourself. "Why me!? Why now!? Bad things always happen to me!"

These are the types of situations that can erupt into nonproductive bouts of anger, anxiety, fear, and self-condemnation, and seriously compromise our judgment and capacity to make healthy and informed decisions.

Indeed, if there's one thing we can predict about human existence, it's that life is unpredictable, filled with inevitable ups and downs. Here's where it's vital to remember that our highly evolved, malleable brains have built-in capacity to intentionally see the glass as *half full* rather than *half empty*. Actively creating stories that align with our core values, central beliefs, and transcendent purpose in life helps us do just this. We always have the choice to view our world through a prism of perspective and acquired wisdom, which brings us directly to the doorstep of making better choices.

Third, our interpretation of the events that occur around us is the vital issue. Here's where the importance of nurturing our genes in a way that builds and fortifies Y.O.D.A. becomes crystal clear. In short, the biological process of gene expression, hormonal and neurotransmitter activity, and other biochemical processes that take place under our skin have less to do with the life events themselves and everything to do with the stories we tell ourselves about what happened and why.

When we reflect, process, frame, and reframe life experiences so they work for us rather than against us, we keep our hands firmly on the proverbial cognitive steering wheel. And this is precisely how we maintain a sense of control when the storms of life are raging. *What's real in the mind is also real in the body* at a molecular level, and the stories we tell ourselves can either help or harm our health and, hence, our decision-making capacity across life.

In the words of Dr. Edith Eger, Auschwitz survivor and renowned inspirational author and speaker, the real payoff comes when we move ourselves from the story of ourselves as victims ("Why me?") to survivors ("What's next?").

Let's take another view of the downside stories previously mentioned through the lens of your trained Inner Voice 2, the acquired wisdom of Y.O.D.A.:

- Your computer crashes. Y.O.D.A. self-coaching advice: "Breathe deeply, reflect on what you can do. Take down a few notes.

It will be an interesting challenge for you to present without your PowerPoint slides. You know the material so well. Maybe you'll be even better with fresh, spontaneous energy? Even if not, you'll have given it your very best shot, which is all that can be expected!"

- You find yourself in a fiery argument that sprang up from nowhere. Y.O.D.A. self-coaching advice: "Take a deep breath and lower your voice. Establish boundaries and make a plan to address the issue later, garnering the needed time and space to collect your thoughts." When you reconnect on the topic of the argument, start your first sentence with "My brain shuts down when I feel attacked. I am overcome by emotions and shut down to protect myself from getting hurt. When we have a hot-button topic that needs our attention, how can address it differently next time to protect us both and solve the problem?"

- Your car dies. Y.O.D.A. self-coaching advice: "Take a deep breath and try to assess the situation as clearly as possible. You're in no danger, so call AAA for help. Call your friend and tell her you'll be a few minutes later, and ask her to have a good glass of wine ready when you arrive. You can handle this!"

By reshaping stories of failure, frustration, and friction into growth-oriented narratives of learning and resilience, we weave multi-colored strands of real-life experience, good and bad, into our reposi-tory of knowledge and wisdom.

Over time, we become aware that the annoying and destabilizing events that used to ruffle us, sometimes derailing our emotional train, are in reality another chance to fortify and train Y.O.D.A. Our adven-turous, unpredictable travels across life's most challenging terrain offer an extraordinary opportunity for learning, growth, and acquired good counsel.

THE SECRET TO NEUROPLASTICITY LIES "ABOVE OUR GENES"

The complex biological process of nurture shaping nature, the study of how our genes are read, transcribed, and expressed, is called "epigenetics," which literally translated means "above the genes." Our genes are the starting ingredients in our recipe for development; epigenetic processes act on our DNA to produce the molecules that shape how we look and feel. Relative to Y.O.D.A. training, and all else in life, it's the things to which we give our full attention and highest-quality energy that, epigenetically speaking, grow strongest over time.

Each time we repeat a behavior or thought that specific neural pathway is coated with a fatty substance called myelin, something that was briefly discussed in Chapter 6. Myelin slowly but surely upgrades the signal strength and speed of transmission of impulses between cells. Forming new habits is simply a matter of myelinating through repetition, dedication, and constant practice.

And the more we myelinate, the more we automate!

Fortifying a direct line to Y.O.D.A.'s timeless wisdom requires building neural circuitry that holds strong in moments of stress, which is analogous to transforming a single-lane neural country road into a six-lane highway. Intentionally investing energy over and over to myelinate and automate instant access to Y.O.D.A. will yield a positive return that's evident in every small, medium, and large decision you make in life.

How Family Life Shapes Who We Become

While wise decision-making is not coded into our genetic makeup, it is coded into our *capability*, when our genes are nurtured in the right way. And inarguably, our first and most powerful context for training a brilliant Y.O.D.A. is at home with our families.

Here's what you need to know.

We learn and grow marinating in the emotional climate established by our parents, a dynamic shaped by the interpersonal chemistry of our own unique family. Clearly, children aren't developmentally equipped to fact-check prevailing attitudes, beliefs, values, ideas, or patterns of behavior of parents or extended family members, particularly in the early years. They watch, learn, and emulate, preparing to one day live their own lives outside of the home and, of course, make their own decisions.

Children are multisensory sponges, integrating both verbal information (words) and equally important nonverbal information (tone, facial expression, body language), modeled by parents and caregivers. Children are constantly searching for cues to guide their development. Telling a child to be polite and respectful to others, then obnoxiously chewing out the hostess because your table isn't ready, is not going to resonate, nor land with the child as something important to remember. Such contradictions virtually *ensure* parental advice in these areas will *not* get uploaded into the child's command center.

"Don't worry that your children aren't listening to you; worry that they are always watching you!" said Robert Fulghum, in a quote that speaks volumes about how child development really happens.

In short, *what you say* is as important as *how you say it*, and when the advice you give to your children is not reflective of your actions, rest assured that access to your child's inner command center will be denied.

Training Y.O.D.A. at Home: The Gift of the Meta-Moment

As human beings, we are as unique as snowflakes, and each in our own way dancing to the sound of our own music. And because we're all different and because our life experiences shape our attitudes and opinions in unique ways, there is no guarantee of a conflict-free ride. In fact, at home, off-guard with the people we love and trust, those who are not supposed to desert us in stressful times, is the easiest place to forget that family members are human too.

This is a perfect training ground for Y.O.D.A.!

Moments of strife with those we love happen to all of us. One second everything's fine, then the next, out of the blue, a seemingly minor event or comment precipitates a rapid drop in the emotional temperature. It's like an arctic front blew into the room, freezing everything up, and each party is suddenly primed for a standoff. There is no rationality or reason, just impulsivity and forcefulness. Underneath it all, a power struggle has erupted and no one wants to budge; everyone wants to win.

But here's the key question. What *is* winning in this scenario?

Termed "meta-moments," these everyday scenarios present fertile opportunities for Y.O.D.A. learning and growth. And in the end, winning is not about being right or wrong, having an opinion or idea validated or not. Rather, victory happens when each party feels heard, respected, and valued, despite differences of opinion or perspective. And gaining this kind of traction is not possible when enmeshed in the chilly, reactive, and inflexible psychological tundra of one's untrained inner voice (Inner Voice 1).

Receiving a message in a tone laced with anger, frustration, or judgment, matching body language and facial expression, nearly guarantees the messages being sent will not be heard. In the same way one can route unwanted email directly into the clutter folder, one can route hostile verbiage into the command center's repository for junk. There's no chance for learning or growth when the message is blocked from the very start.

Here are a few examples of messages destined to be auto-routed into the command center's junk folder:

- Parent to child: "Stop the worthless computer gaming *now!*" Your words are loud and angry, your tone is harsh and inflexible, and your body language is rigid, with the result that your message will likely be **blocked**.

- Sibling to sibling: "That's *my* toy. Give it to me or else!" The words are bossy and possessive, the tone is impatient and frustrated, and the body language is aggressive, with the result that the message will likely be **blocked**.

- Spouse to spouse: "You're so selfish! It's all about you! I deserve better!" Your words are angry and attacking, your tone is punitive and judgmental, and your body language is decidedly negative, with the result that your message is most likely **denied entry**.

Stop and think for a moment. Would you feel heard, respected, and valued as the recipient of messages delivered in this manner?

Now let's explore using your trained inner voice (Inner Voice 2) to repackage, restate, and redeliver the same messages. If the overarching goal is for the intended message to get to get through to the command center of the person, whole and intact, here are some possibilities:

- Parent to child: "I want what's best for you because I love you. I'm concerned that too much screen time will limit your amazing creativity and brain power and dim the brilliant light I know you have inside!"

- Sibling to sibling: "I know you love that toy and have been playing with it for a long time now. I'm feeling frustrated right now because I also want to play with it and you're not letting me! Any chance I can have it when you're all done?"

- Spouse to spouse: "I love you and want to feel close to you, but I feel sad and lonely when you prioritize work over being fully present with me."

The bottom line is that when we intentionally pause, take a deep breath, reflect on what's really going on, and align our message and tone with the best advice from our trained resident advisor, our Y.O.D.A., the action or inaction we then take opens the door to new, exciting learning. Once inside the command center, the messages and insights can germinate into new insights, perspectives, and even gratitude for seeing things now that could not be seen before.

Standing above the fray, watching yourself manage a meta-moment with grace and skill, represents your wisdom in action. You are purposely building neural pathways of healthy discourse both with yourself as well as those with whom you are interacting. And the most important place to bring your wisdom forward (Y.O.D.A.) is with your family. It is precisely here that multigenerational dysfunction can be stopped dead in its tracks.

FROM NOVICE TO EXPERT: CREATING A NEURAL SUPERHIGHWAY

You've digested a great deal of information in this chapter. Now let's make these new ideas and concepts practical and relatable.

Recall a specific time in your life where you transformed a challenging new learning into a well-established habit. It could be something like driving a car where you no longer have to consciously think to enact the desired response, like putting your foot on the brake or looking into your rearview mirror before changing lanes. The new behaviors just happen by themselves. You no longer have to consciously think about what to do because the behaviors have been trained to happen automatically.

Reflect on how the process unfolded and what was required to develop mastery. It is also important to consider how you've managed to keep the skills intact over time.

The Answer: You invested significant effort, energy, and time into both learning the new skill and preserving it. Driving competency, which was challenging and awkward in the beginning, eventually became second nature. Your dedication and commitment to acquire the desired skills have paid big dividends and now you possess an acquired constellation of skills that will aid you throughout your lifetime. And this is the exact process we all must follow to acquire extraordinary competence in our decision-making.

Follow the prompts below to describe how you, perhaps supported by family or friends, could myelinate a specific skill in decision-making. An example could be pausing before important decisions and using your capacity for reflective consciousness to ensure that you are not deceiving yourself to get what you want, that you are seeing all the viable alternatives in the decision, or that you have properly used the seven lens vetting process before deciding.

Assignment:

Describe the decision-making skill you would like to automate, and then explain in some detail how you would convert the desired behavior into a reliable habit—a highly efficient six-lane neural superhighway.

_____

_____

Based on the example you just gave and all that you have learned thus far, the headline should read: *Extraordinary things are possible when you invest your highest-quality effort, energy, and precision in the habits you wish to automate.* Wise decision-making may not be coded in our genes but can, over time, be intentionally uploaded into our daily repertoire, allowing us to steadily move from novice to expert—and that, in short, is a game changer!

PART II

Y.O.D.A. APPLIED TO CHILDREN, TEENS, AND FAMILIES

CHAPTER 8

Y.O.D.A. Rising: Parenting Young Children

I've learned that people will forget what you said, people will forget what you did, but people will never forget how you made them feel.

—Maya Angelou

Now that you understand the power of your inner voice, let's explore the most significant idea of all: how your public voice as a parent becomes the inner voice of your child, shaping the broad underlying themes of how they feel about themselves and the choices they make.

To understand how stories and belief systems cross generations, we will start by reflecting on the genesis of your own untrained Inner Voice 1 and how that voice may be influencing the public voice you use with your child now. More importantly, we will explore how your untrained public voice can be intentionally transformed into a trusted inner coach for your child that will yield priceless decision-making dividends for life. (See Figure 8.1.)

As a parent, you are your child's *first and most powerful teacher*, and just as teachers require formal training in order to provide high-quality lessons to their students, so do parents, particularly if a healthy inner voice was not embedded in you as a growing child.

Wise Decision Insight: One of the greatest gifts you can give to your children is a strong and wise inner voice, a measured and thoughtful decision advisor that will be with them throughout their lifetime, something we refer to as Y.O.D.A. Rising.

The parent-child bond is unlike any other relationship in nature. Implicit trust and complete dependence are central to caregiver-infant

Figure 8.1   Transforming the inner voice.

attachment relationships, not only for a child's healthy development, but for their very survival. It is within the context of this powerful bond that the primary caregiver's words, tone, behavior, and other nonverbal messages set the stage for what will become their fundamental belief systems, habits and behaviors, and competence in decision-making.

The infant brain is a rapidly growing learning machine, one that is built gradually over many years in a dynamic ongoing epigenetic construction process that begins at conception. Simpler neural connections form first, the ones that undergird the communication pathways in the brain for attachment relationships with the primary caregiver, for love, care, feeding, protection, and survival. More complex connections and networks, as well as the crosstalk connectivity between networks, develop later in time for other developmentally important activities such as talking, walking, socializing, reading, writing, and riding a bicycle. The human infant's brain is establishing more than one million new neural connections every second, with the highest priority given to those that increase the child's chances of thriving and survival.

As will be explained more thoroughly in Chapter 11, the things we invest our energy in by paying attention, particularly the things we focus on intently, grow stronger over time. As the primary caregiver, you are the center of the infant's universe, and hence you decide, by your energy investments, the qualities you wish to grow in your child and when.

Giving your attention and energy to love, appreciation, patience, empathy, compassion, kindness, and joy spawns growth and accelerated development in those priceless human capacities. It is under this evolutionary model that caregiver energy investments, evidenced in their stories and embodied in their actions, directly and unquestioningly embed emotions and behaviors that the child automatically emulates, all of which occur under the radar of the child's conscious awareness.

This is nature's way of equipping babies with the emotional tools, cognitive knowledge, and decision-making skills required to survive and thrive later as adults. In the early stages of development, intentional discernment of what and who gains entry into their inner command center is simply not an option for the child. Information taken in from the outside world, in particular from the child's primary caregiver, is like an IV drip directly into the child's brain, as referenced in Chapter 6, programming early neural pathways that form the foundation for all later learning.

All information that passes through the infant's senses (hearing, vision, touch, taste, smell) in their experience of daily life creates and fortifies the neural pathways that become, for that particular individual, communication signals in the brain that represent de facto truth. The more energy that is invested by the mother or father in particular inputs to his or her child, like a loving smile, a warm cuddle, or rapid response to the child's needs, this "serve and return" dynamic of reliable connection fortifies these neural pathways into automated belief systems (I am safe, and I bring my mother and father joy). This felt sense of being lovable and valuable seamlessly becomes the underlying template for a critical inner belief that sits at the very center of our being, across life, as humans.

Just as the city of Rome was built atop a foundation developed centuries ago, the brain builds new learning on top of old, integrating novel information into an existing set of core beliefs. This highly apropos metaphor from neuroscientist David Eagleman is precisely why getting the child's foundation right in the early years is so crucial.

In this context, it's vital to know that the child's memory is not only stored in the structures and networks of the brain, but also throughout the body's viscera, organ systems, and muscles in the form of emotions and sensory information. Your words, and perhaps even more importantly your tone, the soft, high-pitched voice in which mothers speak with their infants—a special language called "motherese"—will be remembered throughout the body, a felt sense of that particular moment in time. Your child remembers, at a subconscious level, the feeling of what it felt like to be in your presence, the most enduring and important recollection of all, persisting long after the concrete memory of your spoken words have faded. (See Figure 8.2.)

Let's pause now for a moment of self-reflection to explore how our own inner voice may have been shaped by implicit and explicit memories of our early childhood via our parent's untrained Public Voice 1. Let's also examine how our command center may benefit from reevaluation to ensure the inner decision-making capacity we are building in our children contains the wisdom of a trusted **coach** rather than the criticism of an unreliable and critical **adversary**.

To explore this multigenerational transmission of powerful unquestioned messages early in life, let's go through a reflection exercise and consider a few pertinent questions to ponder and process:

1. How did your parent's public voice shape your inner voice as a child?

    • Name two important **positive messages** repeatedly conveyed by the parent or the adult who raised you in

Parent (Untrained)	Parent (Trained)
Public Voice 1 to child Inner Voice 1	Public Voice 2 to child Inner Voice 2

Figure 8.2   Tone of voice can convey more than words.

infancy and early childhood (your primary caregiver). How did this data shape your beliefs about the world, your place within it, and your sense of competence, confidence, and self-worth?

- _____
  _____

- _____
  _____

- What are two important **negative messages** from your primary caregiver that shaped your beliefs about the world, your place within it, and your sense of competence, confidence, loveability, and self-worth?

  - _____

  - _____

- If you had to name one key **positive** message that helped you in your life, and one key **negative** message that hindered you, what would they be?

  - Helped: _____

  - Hindered: _____

- As you reflect on these deeply felt messages that shaped your life in powerful ways, which are the ones you **do** want to build and reinforce in your one child's command center? Which are the messages you **do not** want to upload?

  - Yes, Upload! _____

  - Do Not Upload: _____

It is by bringing discipline to your energy investments, by intentionally uploading helpful messages and choosing not to invest your energy in harmful ones, that you can break dysfunctional multigenerational family cycles and initiate a new positive narrative—the story you want yourself and your child to live their way into. With your trained public voice giving rise to a constructive, healthy inner voice, your child's decision-making competencies and skills will be a fundamental part of how they operate in their world—across life.

Let's expand on this reflection exercise by turning to the present day, taking time now to explore key messages and themes you're uploading into your child's highly sensitive, rapidly growing inner command center.

2. How is your present public voice shaping your child's inner voice?

    - List two key messages you are uploading to your child's private inner voice via your public voice. Distinguish between times when you are relaxed and rested, and the emotional climate is stress-free. Conversely, think of the times of exhaustion, household disorder, and crying infants or toddler tantrums.

        - Stress-Free Emotional Climate:

            - 1: _____

            - 2: _____

        - Stressful Emotional Climate:

            - 1: _____

            - 2: _____

3. How are the messages you're embedding into your child's command center similar to or different from the ones your parents uploaded to you?

    - Similar: _____

    - Different: _____

    - Which of these messages are constructive and which are not? What messages do you intend to *continue* to upload and which messages do you want to be certain *not* to upload to your child?

        _____

        _____

        _____

4. Now that you've reflected upon these high-level multigen-erational messages and patterns, let's do some parent-child Y.O.D.A. training. Rising above in the moment from your raw, untrained Public Voice 1 to your best Public Voice 2, especially during times of stress, requires intentional and dedicated practice. For example, being aware of the reality of the moment, such as when your overly tired rascal tod-dler decides to throw their food all over the kitchen—food you've lovingly prepared for them—and embracing the opportunity this situation affords requires presence, insight, and practice. Your response, whether *action* or *reaction*, can upload a strength-building inner coach to your child or a critical inner voice. This is a choice you will have. How should you respond?

- Write about a real-life example from the past week in which you've lost your temper in a stressful moment with your child, one in which you wished you'd **chosen** to handle the situation differently. Which specific words did you use, and in what tone? What message did your body language communicate?

  _____

  _____

  _____

- Now write about the same event and how the sce-nario would have played out had you used your trained Y.O.D.A. to rise above the frustrating details of the moment, **choosing** to show up as your Best Self. What specific words would you use, and in what tone? What message would your body language communicate?

  _____

  _____

  _____

5. Finally, consider three key messages you intend to upload into your child's central command center (their inner voice) that you hope will accompany them as priceless assets in their future decision-making and sense of self-worth.

- _____
- _____
- _____

To recap: Children develop as they do in response to complex environmental inputs, nurture shaping nature all the way along, the full impact of which cannot be wholly known until much later in life, when they are well into adulthood. Those who are closest to the child, those who are in the best position to control what gets uploaded into their command center, have the greatest opportunity to powerfully shape the multidimensional health, happiness, character, and inner wisdom of the child, giving them the best possible odds of expressing their full human potential in their life.

Bottom line: **A healthy multigenerational family story begins with an intentionally trained _you_.**

CHAPTER 9

High-Performance Training for Parents: Y.O.D.A. for Teens

Being a young person in today's day and age is as stressful and challenging as almost any time in recent history. Navigating the social landscape in the context of COVID-19, surging hormones, cognitive impulsivity, and self-conscious developmental awkwardness clearly presents an exceedingly slippery slope for parents of teens.

When we factor in the ubiquitous and addictive nature of screens and social media, as habit forming as illicit drugs or gambling, the constant uploading of anxiety-provoking messages related to social inclusion and perfection, combined with verbal and nonverbal messages from parents and teachers related to high performance and achievement, it's clear that this is not a recipe for sustained healthy adolescent development!

What's also clear is that protecting our children's mental health and mind-body well-being by strengthening their Y.O.D.A. has *never been more important* than it is today.

Parenting during adolescence requires a markedly different skill set than that required during the early years of development. Your teen is well past the high chair, rapidly growing into their independence, expressing their individuality in unique and colorful ways. They are now fully verbal and using their language skills in ways that at times feel like a blessing and others like a curse.

This brand-new communication landscape for parents and teens is laden with joy and angst, productivity and pitfalls, celebrated achievements and sheer unadulterated frustration. As emotional hormone-driven rollercoasters of uncontrollable highs and lows, teens are doing exactly what they're supposed to at this age and stage. Adolescence is the age where, if development is following a typical course, they challenge the status quo, push the boundaries, and begin the journey of discovering who they are now and who they want to be in life.

It's important to note that teenage developmental chaos is not all bad. In this churn of self-discovery, brain development, and biologic recalibration lies a massive opportunity for learning, growth, innovation, and expression of remarkable human potential. The following excerpt from Robert Sapolsky's excellent book *Behave: The Biology of Humans at Our Best and Worst*, from the chapter titled "Adolescence; or, Dude, Where's My Frontal Cortex?" captures adolescence brilliantly:

"Think about this—adolescence and early adulthood are the times when someone is most likely to kill, be killed, leave home forever, invent an art form, help overthrow a dictator, ethnically cleanse a village, devote themselves to the needy, become addicted, marry outside their group, transform physics, have hideous fashion taste, break their neck recreationally, commit their life to God, mug an old lady, or be convinced that all of history has converged to make this moment the most consequential, the most fraught with peril and promise, the most demanding that they get involved and make a difference. In other words, it's the time of life of maximal risk taking, novelty seeking, and affiliation with peers."

Does this description resonate with parents of teens? Typical hallmarks of the adolescent years are impulsivity, defensiveness, moodiness, intransigence, and poor judgment, driven largely by the developmental disconnect between the neural networks that shape social-emotional behavior and those that underpin rational, higher-order, integrated thinking.

As covered in the Chapter 8, humans develop social skills first for evolutionary purposes (survival), while the neural pathways for attention, emotion regulation, and executive function develop much *later*.

Figure 9.1   Neuroplasticity unfolds rapidly earlier in life.

Executive function, abstract thinking, and reasoning capabilities unfold across life, though in a more significant way through our late 20s and early 30s. Our brains are continually growing and evolving, creating new neural connections based on life experiences and atrophying those we no longer need or use. (See Figure 9.1.) This epigenetic remodeling, called "neuroplasticity," is an ongoing process throughout life, markedly more rapid during the earlier stages (childhood, adolescence, and early adulthood) relative to middle age and elderhood.

Similar to early infancy and childhood, the teen years are a known "sensitive period" where the brain is the most highly malleable and open to new habit formation than at any other time across life. This means that adolescence is a potential high-return-on-investment (ROI) developmental window when new learning has much greater odds for lifelong uploading into your teen's long-term memory, where it sticks for good. That is, if the message can get through to their inner command center!

While inputs into the recipe for your teen's long-term healthy development are vast and extensive, by far the most important ingredients for ensuring long-term success will come from *you*. It is you who have the unique and priceless opportunity to shape their habits, beliefs, and behaviors during a developmental period of time that is unlike all others.

By living your message and modeling good judgment, particularly in times laden with stress or conflict, and by practicing disciplined self-care to sustain balanced mental, emotional, physical, and spiritual health, you can begin to steadily embed a trusted and reliable inner coach that can protect them from the downside of life-altering bad decisions.

Rising up into the reflective consciousness of Y.O.D.A. is the first necessary step in transporting you knowingly above the complexities of a situation brewing on the ground. And it's only from this higher-level vantage point that we can *see what's really happening*. When we're not enmeshed in the heated emotions of the moment, insights can begin to surface, observations that empower you to see that the spirited pushback from your teen is not personal. Rather, they are testing the boundaries you've established, something that is completely in line with their healthy growth and development.

Reframing teen intransigence that appears to be an all-out affront of willful disrespect and disregard, and doing this at a powerful teachable moment, can, if managed correctly, embed a sticky life-changing lesson, and not *despite* the emotional charge of the moment, but rather *because* of it. All meaningful learning involves emotion, and we are much likelier to remember events that have significant emotional valence. And when your wise and skillful Y.O.D.A. situation management deescalates a moment that could easily have felt doused with emotional kerosene, all of a sudden this moment becomes a shared experience of learning and growth, where both you and your child can see each other as human beings and can begin to chart a healthy course forward.

A simple reflective pause, one that brings you calmness and perspective in a meta-moment, can change everything for you and for your ornery teen. Modeling Y.O.D.A. in a heated moment is, bar none, the most powerful way you can teach them how to thoughtfully and skillfully manage their own difficult, emotionally charged life situations in the future. A gift of epic proportions!

Your refusal to become defensive and attacking, and your willingness to listen and stay positively engaged, will unknowingly be uploaded into their repository of Y.O.D.A. learning. The gate to your teen's inner command center will likely open because they know, deep inside, you love them and always have their best interests at heart. As should be obvious by this point, we most effectively convey important lessons not by harsh, heavy-handed punitive messaging but rather by subtly sliding in lessons below the radar of conscious awareness, not only by *what we say* but *how we say it*. It is *our being what we want them to be* that carries the most powerful Y.O.D.A. message and lesson.

Wise Decision Insight: All emotionally charged challenges in life, particularly the painful ones, represent fertile ground for Y.O.D.A. learning in the areas of emotional control, perspective, and sound judgment.

In summary, as the primary adult in your teen's life, your words and tone matter more in terms of long-term health and development than most people ever suspected. The old adage "sticks and stones may break my bones, but words will never hurt me" is diametrically opposed to cutting-edge research on the impact of repeated hurtful language, particularly in the case of young children. (See Figure 9.2.)

It's important to understand that neuroscience research has demonstrated that the brain interprets emotional pain as *equivalent* to

Parent (Untrained)	Parent (Trained)
Public Voice 1 to teen Inner Voice 1	Public Voice 2 to teen Inner Voice 2

Figure 9.2   Contrary to the old saying, words can have a powerful impact.

physical pain. This finding has broad ramifications for us as parents in our efforts to safeguard the spiritual, mental, emotional, and physical well-being of our children and massive implications for the mental health crisis in our country and world. As you learned in Chapter 7, what's real in the mind is also real in the body at a molecular level, and this is a central tenet that we must all understand and hold close. Optimal mind-body health requires disciplined and diligent self-care, which is the foundation for wise decision-making and all else in life.

Time for Reflection and Y.O.D.A. Goal-Setting

Here are a few exercises designed to help build the awareness and skills required to leverage teachable moments effectively with your teen, particularly the emotionally charged, stressful situations that seemingly spring up out of nowhere, impacting both your mood and that of your child and infusing negative energy into the home.

Reflect on the following questions for you and your teen. If you have more than one child, please reflect on each one individually. Remember, we humans are like snowflakes: No two are exactly alike, not even identical twins!

1. Write down two of the most significant areas of difficulty with your teen (e.g. technology use, cleaning up after themselves, homework).

    • _____

    _____

    • _____

    _____

2. Write down two or three major areas in your home where difficult conversations about these topics tend to occur (e.g. kitchen, bedroom, television area), and consider the times of day when conflict is likeliest to arise (e.g. dinner time).

    • _____

    • _____

3. Name one situation between you and your teen over the past week that entailed a hot-button topic. How did you handle it, and was the situation resolved? Was there any forward movement? How did your teen respond, and how did you feel afterward?

_____

_____

_____

_____

SUCCESS FOR ALL: ENGAGING Y.O.D.A.

Being aware of the major hot-button topics and both *when* as well as *under what circumstances* they're likely to occur is step 1. Advance preparation is key! Knowing your major learning and teaching goals will help you stay alert for meta-moments, connecting the dots of opportunity when the moment is upon you, vastly improving your odds of success.

Now let's visualize, reflect, and write. In the blank space below, recast the story of the challenging parent-teen interaction with your Y.O.D.A. in charge and in high gear, listing the time, topic, situation, and physical location, *seeing and feeling* the 360-degree picture of the event before it unfolds. You are the leader, the agent of change, embodying wisdom in action, making thoughtful, wise, and balanced decisions that guide you and your teen to a constructive long-term outcome.

_____

_____

_____

_____

_____

This vision is indeed possible with Y.O.D.A. practice. And if you need motivation to double down on building those neural pathways, here it is. By the time your teen graduates from high school, it's estimated that 93% of the time you'll ever spend with them across their entire life is now in the rearview mirror. It is a sobering statistic, but think about it: Once they go off to college, get their first jobs, and eventually have families of their own, your opportunity to strengthen their Y.O.D.A. and decision-making skills is vastly reduced.

So let's double down on your Y.O.D.A. training game plan to move toward the healthy, happy, connected, and loving relationship you aspire to with your teenager. While bumpy at times, the mutual respect and the knowledge that together you will find a way are hallmarks of this new way of being human together.

By showing up as your own Y.O.D.A. Best Self, you are actively and intentionally uploading decision-making expertise not only to your teen, but throughout your entire family, given the ripple effect of emotions. You are seamlessly embedding the priceless gift of wisdom into the command center of your most precious asset, your child, a leader in the rising generation and the steward of your family legacy. It is a gift they are sure to pay forward.

CHAPTER 10

Transforming Your Family Story with Your Trained Inner Voice

Y.O.D.A. is a powerful tool in establishing a new 2.0 family narrative, whether change is merely a few tweaks to an otherwise healthy story or it breaks a seemingly intractable negative multigenerational cycle. By accessing our wise and trusted trained Inner Voice 2 to manage family dynamics in ways that promote mutual respect, heartfelt dialogue, understanding, and unconditional love, we can write and then live our way into the updated narratives we choose and deserve.

By introducing healthy new behaviors, mindsets, and traditions into the family milieu, we infuse a new and improved sense of togetherness, the joy and comfort of what it means to be a cohesive family. The goal: managing difficult decisions, arguments, differences of opinion, emotional flares, and other typically challenging family dynamics in a flexible, adaptive manner, rather than being entrenched in the black-and-white rigidity that characterizes families in which the next emotional eruption is one inadvertent comment or innocent overlook away.

Any way you slice it, parenting is hard work, and markedly more so for those whose childhoods were marked by unresponsive caregiving, emotional turbulence, lack of safety, or trauma. But here's the good news. Despite childhood adversity, as pointed out in previous chapters, our brains are dynamically rewiring each moment of every day, at all ages and stages across life. This means that even if your childhood was marked by disruption and instability, there's an ever-present opportunity to change your story, to intentionally create a new and empowering narrative of possibility, human connection, and transformation that can profoundly reshape the path forward for all of the individuals within the family system.

By examining our harmful autopilot behaviors, attitudes, and beliefs that were absorbed into our decision-making command center without question or censorship early in life—particularly the ones that bring nothing but heartache, disconnection, disruption, and despair—we can establish a new strategic Y.O.D.A. path. This route allows us to transform a story of adversity, perhaps even one of multi-generational trauma, into one of post-traumatic growth for ourselves, our children, and all generations to follow.

"There is a crack in everything. That's how the light gets in."

—Leonard Cohen

Transformation is only possible when we can create an emotionally safe shared energy space, which can only happen when we have the wisdom and agency to act rather than react. When we seek to understand, perspective-share, and empathize, without blaming or shaming, we create a fertile emotional climate that makes it possible to see and internalize things that simply weren't possible to comprehend and take in before, no matter how challenging and disruptive the subject matter may have been relative to one's long-held beliefs. We can recognize that differences of opinion need not be taken as a personal affront, rather simply accept the fact that even family members can have radically different points of view and belief systems.

In this updated 2.0 narrative of hope and possibility, we lean into the challenges of family life by training in the Y.O.D.A. home gym to develop adaptive skills, mindsets, and behaviors that result *only because of* the inevitable struggles of family life. The ripple effect of your thoughtful and steady leadership during turbulent times instills dynamic, growth-fueled energy into each person's capacity and confidence to make responsible and wise decisions. This competency is built within the family system, and extends to the broader arena of life.

Armed with this knowledge, the home becomes the most important classroom for critical Y.O.D.A. learning. By reframing adversity as an opportunity to learn and grow, the emotional gridlock of a meta-moment can be leveraged to build multidimensional inner strength, built-in capacities that will inevitably lead to smarter, more informed, and responsible choices later in life. By demonstrating calmness, perspective, and wisdom in moments of crisis within the family, you become living proof that emotional control and responsible decision-making under duress is indeed possible.

Breaking old dysfunctional ways of responding to the storms of family life is certainly challenging. It requires disuse and atrophy of well-trafficked neural highways that are not serving us well, which give rise to impulsivity, rationalization, and intense anger. By not investing our energy in the dysfunctional habits we no longer want or need, while simultaneously engaging and reengaging in the effortful work of building new habits, we can build more adaptive neural pathways that serve us rather than stop us, mind-body communication systems that are aligned with our deepest values and aspirations.

While science is clear that change is possible across life, uploading positive habits and mindsets in childhood and adolescence is always easier and more efficient than unlearning unhelpful or harmful behaviors in adulthood. When parents and caregivers lead with their Inner Voice 2 and Public Voice 2 from the beginning, your 2.0 family story can be activated *from the very start!*

THE RECIPE FOR UPSHIFTING YOUR FAMILY STORY

Step 1: Develop awareness. Think of a situation in the last month where you responded in a way that did not serve you or family members well. After considerable reflection, how could you have responded differently? How could you have responded that would be more aligned with your core values and best decision-making self? Write down the OLD dysfunctional response, the one you want to eliminate with disuse, and the NEW learned response you will actively strengthen with repeated use.

- OLD: I will atrophy/extinguish:

_____

_____

_____

_____

_____

- NEW: I will strengthen/automate:

_____

_____

_____

_____

_____

Step 2: Create your Y.O.D.A. Code. Now that you're aware of both the behavior you aim to atrophy (OLD) and the one you will strengthen and replace (NEW), let's create your Y.O.D.A. Code. In the meta-moments of our everyday family life, having clear and concrete reminders of how we want to respond when the emotional climate suddenly freezes up can be immensely helpful in summoning the wisdom and perspective of Y.O.D.A.

Scan the following list and circle the words that best capture the spirit and essence of the vision you have for yourself. Then write 10 words in the space provided that best describe who you want to be in times of family crisis.

Note: This process will take longer than one sitting. Furthermore, your Y.O.D.A. Code will likely change over time as you evolve, grow, refine, and learn.

Possibilities for Your Y.O.D.A. Code

Adaptable	Discerning	Morally	Respectful
Adventurous	Empathic	courageous	Challenge
Affectionate	Engaging	Moral	seeking
Ambitious	Focused	integrity	Self-aware
Authentic	Forgiving	Motivated	Self-control/
Compassionate	Generous	Open-	Willpower
Competitive	Grateful	minded	Tough-minded/
Confident	Honorable	Optimistic	Mentally tough
Creative	Humble	Organized	Trusting
Critical	Funny/	Patient	Truthful/
thinker	Humorous	Personally	Honest
Curious	Just	courageous	Vital/Vigorous
Decisive	Kind/Loving	Positive	Wise
Dependable	Lifelong	Prudent	Altruistic
Determined/	learner	Punctual	Open-minded
Gritty	Loyal	Resilient	Playful/Fun

After reflecting one more time on the words that truly resonate with you, write down the 10 words that best describe who you
aspire to be when family storms erupt. These are the finalists for your
Y.O.D.A Code.

1. _____

2. _____

3. _____

4. _____

5. _____

6. _____

7. _____

8. _____

9. _____

10. _____

From your list of 10 finalists, select 5 and write them in the circle graphic in Figure 10.1. This is your Y.O.D.A. Code, your lifeline to activating your trained resident advisor.

Step 3: Post your Y.O.D.A. Code. Make your Y.O.D.A. Code easily visible in areas where you're most likely to be challenged, such as in your kitchen, dining room, or bedroom. Place reminders in as many strategic places as possible. The more reminders you have, the more lifelines you will have to the treasure trove of Y.O.D.A. wisdom and perspective.

Step 4: Recognize the meta-moment. "This is it! This is what I've been training for!" Seize the emotionally charged moment to initiate your training and summon your best envisioned self. This difficult moment is simply one more opportunity to practice, improve, and demonstrate your wisdom skills.

Step 5: Practice, practice, practice! Build a six-lane neural highway that takes you directly to the wisdom of Y.O.D.A., whenever and wherever the storms of family life descend. Private Voice 2 and Inner Voice 2 should be immediately activated.

Step 6: Make Y.O.D.A. journal entries. Write down the details of any event that unfolded during the day where you consciously practiced accessing Y.O.D.A. and your best public and private voice. What were the circumstances? How did the meta-moment

Figure 10.1   Five Y.O.D.A. Code words.

start? What helped and what blocked the best version of yourself from showing up? Was the outcome positive or negative? What did you learn?

By following steps 1–6, slowly but surely your old, outdated, dead-end inner voice will weaken with disuse, your wise inner voice will steadily strengthen, and your ability to constructively manage family crises will exponentially improve.

Bottom line: To transform your family narrative, you must become the change you want to see, and you must learn emotion regulation strategies to model wise and thoughtful responses, even in the darkest moments of family life.

Wise Decision Insight: We, as parents, set the bar and we, as parents, always start with *ourselves*.

PART III

Y.O.D.A. IN THE BROADER ARENA OF LIFE

CHAPTER 11

Managing Energy and Your Inner Voice

Energy, not time, is your most precious resource. Success in life will not be measured by the number of years you lived, but rather by the energy you brought to the time you had, aligned with what mattered most to you while we were here.

Energy infuses life into time, and the union of energy and time is what makes everything happen in life. Every one of the 30 trillion cells in the human body has its own energy production plant called the mitochondria, and cellular energy production is what ignites life in the human system. And human energy, like all energy in the universe, possesses quantity, quality, focus, and intensity (force). Here's the critical insight:

Energy investment spawns life, and one's inner voice controls energy investment.

Let's start with these energy fundamentals. Making a conscious effort to do something means intentionally investing your energy in that activity. Making a conscious effort to strengthen your biceps by lifting weights is an example. The critical ingredient in the growth-stimulating process is **energy investment**. Spending time in the gym but failing to invest targeted energy into building your bicep will not get the job done. This same principle is true with everything, such as investing your energy in being a good parent, improving your back-hand in tennis, or growing your capacity for kindness or gratefulness. And the greater the quantity, quality, focus, and intensity of the energy invested, the greater the chance that growth will be spawned.

103

Intentionally investing one's full and best energy is called **full engagement** and represents the real sweet spot of human energy. To be fully engaged means you're *all in*, investing the greatest quantity, highest quality, most precise focus, and greatest intensity of energy, right here, right now. Showing up fully engaged is the greatest gift we have to give to the world because of its direct connection to expanded growth. In other words, when we take energy (life) from our body and invest it elsewhere, we give life and the potential for growth to whomever or whatever we've chosen to give our energy. The central connection of all this to managing your energy and strengthening your Y.O.D.A., is that your inner voice is the master controller of all your energy investments. Your private inner voice ultimately determines who or what you will give life energy to, and the quantity, quality, focus, and intensity of the energy invested.

Two Important Dimensions of Energy

Examining energy through a two-dimensional lens provides important insights in managing energy relative to sound decision-making. The two dimensions are *energy intensity* and *energy valence*. Energy intensity, sometimes referred to as force, can range from low intensity to high intensity, and energy valence refers to whether the energy is positive or negative. Another way to think about energy valence is whether the energy feeling state is perceived as pleasant or unpleasant. The two-dimensional model creates four cells (see Figure 11.1):

- High Positive

- Low Positive

- High Negative

- Low Negative

Common feelings associated with each of the four energy cells are shown in Figure 11.2.

Reflect for a moment on the decisions you have made when you were in a high negative energy state, when you are angry, anxious,

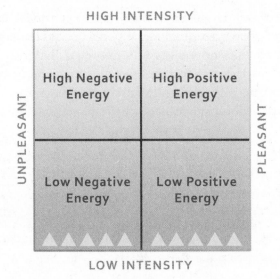

Figure 11.1 The four cells of energy dimensions.

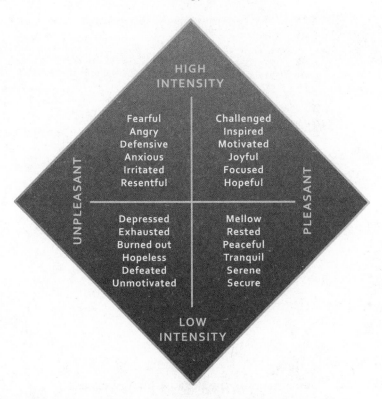

Figure 11.2 The feelings connected to each energy cell.

resentful, or afraid. How about low negative energy? Were you able to make good, sound decisions when you were depressed, exhausted, feeling burned out, hopeless, or unmotivated? Most report that a state of high or low negative energy can seriously compromise their decision-making process. Most also report that wise, time-less decisions are best made in either high positive or low positive energy cells.

This is precisely where reflective consciousness becomes critical. Acknowledging which energy cell you're in prior to making important decisions is essential information for Y.O.D.A. to consider in the delib-eration process.

The takeaway here is this: Except in cases of immediate threats to your survival, postpone, delay, or change your negative energy state before making important decisions. (See Figure 11.3.)

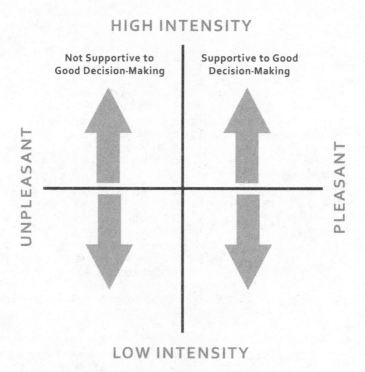

Figure 11.3   Understanding the negative energy state.

Some Additional Wise Decision Insights to Consider

High negative energy states are essentially survival based and consume high levels of our energy reserves. Intense anger, fear, resentment, and the like can produce high levels of adrenocortical hormones such as cortisol, epinephrine, and norepinephrine, which not only can compromise our judgment and decision-making, but can be very harmful to our overall health over time.

The point here is not to demonize negative energy states. There is an appropriate time and place for all emotions and their outward-facing counterpart of our feelings, as long as we can understand the messages being sent and then move forward to constructively adapt to whatever challenges we face. Chronic exposure to high negative energy states will eventually drain our energy reserves, leading to low negative energy *for survival purposes*. Low energy states like exhaustion, hopelessness, depression, or feeling burned out often represent the body's effort to protect you by forcing you into a badly needed recovery mode.

Figure 11.4 depicts the tendency for chronic high negative energy states to unknowingly move you toward low energy. This represents a survival strategy by the body to restore strength in order to prevent long-term damage.

A healthier and more adaptive alternative is to break chronic negative energy states with voluntary recovery. (See Figure 11.5.)

Low positive energy is the quadrant in the energy figure that holds healing and recovery. This represents energy restoration and renewal. It is the quadrant of mind-body regeneration. Music, meditation, breathwork, tai chi, nature walks, massage, prayer, quality time with loved ones, sports participation, and creative painting are just a few of the ways one can voluntarily seek recovery.

Wise Decision Insight: Get to the positive side of your energy valence before making important life decisions. Use voluntary recovery to get the energy balance right before making big choices. Energy is a result of self-care and good health, and as you recall from Chapter 1, it is our health that ignites our wisdom in decision-making.

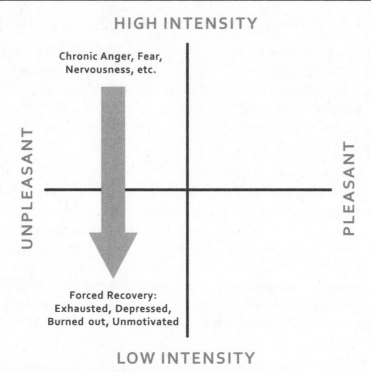

Figure 11.4   Movement from high to low intensity.

Y.O.D.A. Energy Management Basics

- The amount of energy that can be stored in the human body is limited, and we therefore must be very discriminating and purposeful in our energy investments. Y.O.D.A. must constantly advise our inner voice on when and where energy investments should be made in alignment with our highest priorities in life.

- The healthier you are physically, emotionally, mentally, and spiritually, the more energy is typically available for investment, hence the better your decisions. Because cellular energy production occurs fundamentally in the union of oxygen and glucose, issues of nutritional input and aerobic as well as anaerobic fitness are particularly important in both health and sound choices.

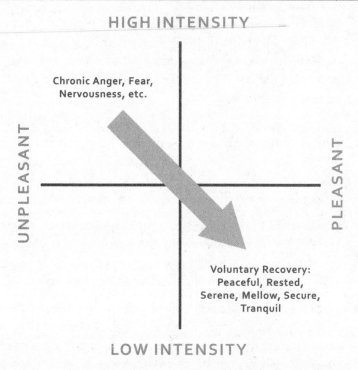

HIGH INTENSITY

Chronic Anger, Fear,
Nervousness, etc.

UNPLEASANT

PLEASANT

Voluntary Recovery:
Peaceful, Rested,
Serene, Mellow, Secure,
Tranquil

LOW INTENSITY

Figure 11.5   Voluntary recovery assists in disrupting negative energy.

- You are the sum total of your energy investments thus far in your life, whether they are intentional or not. Follow your energy! If you have given abundant energy to impatience, sarcasm, victimhood, or cynicism, that's precisely what you've gotten back. Investments in hope, courage, reality-based thinking, honesty, or compassion will spawn vastly different areas of growth. Investments in strengthening your decision-making skills will pay dividends for a lifetime.

- Our ancestors had to develop a conservation of energy bias to ensure survival when food and shelter were scarce. Energy investment was restricted to only those activities that increased their chances for survival. That same conservation bias continues today, regardless of whether food, water, or shelter are abundantly available. A transcendent life purpose, a purpose beyond one's self-interest, and enduring core values open the carefully guarded vault to our energy reserves. When Y.O.D.A. is preloaded with critical operating instructions regarding purpose and values, it can provide judicious and discerning energy investment decisions.

- Human beings are complex, multidimensional energy systems, and the ordering principle for the entire energy system is purpose. Our enduring life purpose can work to order and prioritize our energy investments throughout life. The senior officer in charge of investments is our inner voice.

- Training Y.O.D.A. to move from time literacy to energy literacy, from time awareness to energy awareness, from managing time to managing energy, represents a quantum leap in expanding perspective and wisdom in decision-making.

- Life begins with energy's first pulse and ends with its last. Nothing happens until energy causes something to move. If we want something to weaken or die, we must cut off its energy supply; we simply must not go there with our energy. Atrophy or death is the consequence of cutting off the energy supply to our brain and body. With great counsel, we can make wise and thoughtful energy decisions about what to strengthen and grow and what we intentionally allow to atrophy and die.

- High negative and low negative energy states can completely compromise our capacity for making sound judgments and wise decisions. Every effort should be made to delay decision-making until we can access states of high positive or low positive energy.

"Mindfulness is the awareness that arises through paying attention, on purpose, in the present moment, nonjudgmentally."

—Dr. John Kabat-Zinn

CHAPTER 12

Managing Emotions and the Role of Y.O.D.A.

Our *emotions* and their outward-facing counterparts, our *feelings*, are an ancient and powerful form of information stored and sensed in both the brain and the body. They can be understood and expressed in verbal and nonverbal ways, and in fact are a formidable language of their own. Far from soft and ephemeral, both positive and negative emotions, the bodily messages that give rise to our feelings, when used wisely, must be considered hard, actionable data in decision-making. Evolutionary forces spanning hundreds of thousands of years have equipped our brains and bodies, when properly trained, to recognize, understand, and manage our emotions, interpret them, and use this important data to shape and fine-tune our day-to-day choices.

Ever have a strong "gut feel" about an issue? Something that created a subliminal pull in your stomach, a sensed intuition about a particular life event unfolding in real time? You may have pondered for a moment whether it meant anything or whether it was simply a random sensation related to something you just ate or drank.

This "emotional nudge" has been referred to as your "second brain" talking to you, providing information that, in mentally healthy individuals, should not be casually dismissed. In fact, it is precisely this kind of felt and sensed information that is now becoming widely recognized as vital in augmenting our ability to arrive at the best and most important decisions.

In today's world, this internally sensed neurological and physiological asset is referred to as "emotional intelligence," a term first coined by psychologists Peter Salovey and John Meyer in the 1990s. They define emotional intelligence as "the ability to monitor one's own and other people's emotions, to discriminate between different emotions and label them appropriately, and to use emotional information to guide thinking and behavior."

To this, we would add a fourth category: to aid in **sound decision-making**.

To briefly summarize the science, emotions are the *internal bodily* representations that *underlie feelings*, subconscious biochemical mind-body states associated with thoughts, behaviors, and life circumstances. The sensory experience of emotions falls into two general categories. First, there are those basic bodily urges that have to do with *homeostatic maintenance* of our mind-body system, such as *I'm hungry, I'm thirsty, I'm too hot or too cold, I need to exercise and move my body, I'm exhausted and need to go to sleep.* Second, there are emotions that are *provoked* by an event in the outside world, such as *joy, sadness, fear, contempt, compassion, admiration, jealousy,* and *envy.* All of these emotions, which initiate in our bodies, are experienced by us as feelings.

In short, feelings are our *conscious real-time interpretation* of our embodied emotions, and stem from the particulars of the event itself and how previous life experience has shaped our perspective on what the event means. To paraphrase and extend on this scientific truth, our feelings are the first conscious expression of our emotions, our first and earliest chance to make adaptive meaning of them so that we can employ our Y.O.D.A. skills *to act rather than react.*

Knowing something about where emotions and feelings are located in the brain sheds light on the fundamental yet synergistic differences between these two data sources and how they are indelibly interwoven into our everyday decisions. Although there is some geographic overlap in the neurobiological origins of our emotions and feelings, the vast majority of these two interrelated and synergistic data sources emanate from and are processed in *different parts of the brain.*

Emotions stem from our survival-oriented evolutionarily old subcortical regions of the brain such as the hypothalamus, which regulates the homeostatic balance in our system, as well as the primally focused amygdala, which regulates the fight, flight, or freeze response. Feelings, on the other hand, develop over time as nurture (life experience) shapes nature (our DNA and biochemistry) as we make meaning of the events in our lives, and emanate from our higher-order thought processing networks. Feelings, most importantly, provide the **deliberations** so crucial in sound decision-making.

The neural engines of feelings are centered in the prefrontal cortex, insula, nucleus accumbens, as well as other brain structures in our executive control network that develop and manifest into our thoughts, actions, and behavior. Remember, the integration of our neural networks that set the stage for the self-regulation needed for thoughtful multilevel processing isn't fully developed till our late 20s or early 30s. It is this still-under-construction element of the adolescent brain that explains why teenagers' feelings are *big*, impulsively expressed, and more often than not in vibrant 3-D technicolor and at high volume.

To recap, emotions emanate from the viscera in our bodies and organ systems, the neural wiring dispersed throughout our cellular infrastructure. Emotions are part of our fundamental survival-oriented evolutionary wiring. Feelings, on the other hand, are shaped over time, sculpted by experience. As we live our lives, all the while thinking and interpreting the relevance and meaning of particular situations, we instinctively begin labeling events as good, bad, or indifferent. Recognizing, processing, and expressing feelings can be complex, highly nuanced, and, at times, contradictory and confusing. Human beings are complicated creatures, a timeless fact that plays out in all of our lives each and every day, whether we like it or not.

For example, the *feeling* of seeing a good friend achieve a coveted goal you've been unable to reach, despite your dedicated work and energy investment, may initially elicit the *emotion* of envy. This may be experienced in our body as a constriction of breathing, a headache, or a tightness in the stomach area. In short, an emotional response drives a change of physical state at a molecular level that signals something important is going on that requires attention.

Simultaneously, cross-talk between feelings-related brain centers and bodily viscera can produce an array of complex and perhaps conflicting *feelings*. This is what reveals itself in our conscious minds, whether we reveal it outwardly or not. In this case, you feel joy for your friend, pride that you've been her biggest cheerleader when times were tough and that she's worked tirelessly and effortfully to achieve success. But at the same time, there's a low-lying stream of self-directed anger in having failed to accomplish the very same goal yourself, perhaps even shame that at some level, you feel jealous. You want to feel happy for her, but you're not sure what to do with the embarrassing feeling of jealousy, which is at present the feeling with the strongest signal size.

"Aren't I supposed to be happy for her? What does it mean about me that it's not pure joy I feel? Am I a bad person for feeling jealous?" And just like that, in the flash of a moment, an inner existential conflict arises that we need to settle. This limbo state feels bad inside and out, like mind-body gridlock. What to do?

To complicate things further, you've been asked to coordinate a big celebration for her stunning achievement, and need to make a decision about whether you want to take the helm or leave it to someone else. Making this decision responsibly and authentically demonstrates how challenging it can be to make the right call.

Your untrained inner voice (Inner Voice 1) may be saying, "Not only did she achieve the goal when I've failed, but now I have to lead a celebration of her success too!?" But your trained voice has a different perspective. After summoning your Y.O.D.A. and reflecting on how you might think of this a month, a year, or a decade from now, your trained Inner Voice (Inner Voice 2) sees the bigger picture. Using a 360-degree perspective, your envy and jealousy start losing their pull, and your big heart and true admiration for your friend begin to surface. And your response?

Viewing the situation through the seven lenses, starting from the requisite launch point of balanced mental, emotional, physical, and spiritual health, you begin to process your decision methodically, in order to land on a choice that will serve you and your friend the best over the long game of life. Here's the inner conversation that takes place, and the reflective writing that goes hand in hand.

The Seven Lens Process: Case in Point

1. Best Self: "My Best Self shows up for the people I love in the most empathic, grateful, caring, and humble way I can,

especially in challenging circumstances. I'm not perfect and I drop the ball sometimes, but when I think of this situation a month or a year from now, I'll be proud of how I managed myself to show up for my friend. This will generate positive energy for us both."

2. Best Moral Self: "Celebrating my friend is the right thing to do. It would be small of me not to step up and fully express my love and admiration for her. She really is extraordinary!"

3. Life Purpose: "As someone who strives in general to make the world a better place, I know that in celebrating my friend in an unabashedly loving, caring, thoughtful way, and organizing an event that allows others to celebrate her too, the energy created will be exponential, vastly greater than it could possibly be otherwise. And this positive energy will ripple out to the world in a way that pays it forward to others in the process."

4. Tombstone Legacy: "When my time comes, the words that describe how I'd like to be remembered by those who know me best include these: Kind, Humble, Grateful, Generous, Person of Integrity, Courageous."

5. Core Values and Beliefs: "Showing up, how I carry myself in life and how I reveal who I am through acts of selflessness, honor, and character are, in a word, everything to me."

6. Personal Credo: "I support and protect human beings, and do my best to help them see their brilliant light and live their way into extraordinary life stories they'd never have thought possible. I'm helping my friend to do precisely this!"

7. Ultimate Mission in Life: "When I leave this earth, I want the world to be a more loving, healthier, happier, and more equitable place because of the many opportunities I had to engage in a way that allowed me to make a difference in the lives of others."

Voilà! Here you are, sometime later, balanced and clear-minded, having vetted a tricky downward-pulling emotional nudge in a thoughtful and wise manner through the seven lenses of your most important values and beliefs. This 360-degree reflection set the stage for a decision that couldn't possibly be clearer.

"Yes, *of course* I want to celebrate my friend, and I want to do so in a way that she remembers forever, being held, supported, and loved by her closest friends and family members!" After careful consideration of all your complex feelings, you've consciously decided to take action based on who you most want to be in life, consistent with your deepest values and core purpose for living. This feels both good and right, and allows you to sleep soundly and not look back. You showed up!

Complicated? Yes! But the key here is that the hands you instructed to control your decision-making steering wheel were not the impulsive, emotion-driven feelings of envy and jealousy. This is what Y.O.D.A. is all about: acknowledging all the feelings you might have, then after thorough reflection and processing, deciding what is the right thing to do for you.

A Deeper Dive into Emotions and Feelings

It's not a stretch to say that the push and pull between complex emotions, and the feelings they give rise to, got us to where we are as a human species. Per neuroscientist Antonio Damasio, "Feelings, and all else that relates to being human, lie on a continuum with extremes at either end. . . . Life as we know it is not viable at either extreme."

Early in emotion research, it was believed there were only six primary states: happiness, sadness, fear, disgust, anger, and surprise, but sophisticated biosocial scientists have since discovered this simplistic picture was but the tip of the iceberg. In truth, emotions are highly nuanced and there are many, and most frequently we experience not just one at one time but many simultaneously. (See Figure 12.1 for a representation of the basic relationship between emotions and feelings.)

Feeling sleepy, motivated, exhausted, cheerful, loving, annoyed, irritated, compassionate, excited, uneasy, nervous, hopeful, energized, hopeless, and ecstatic are all everyday examples of complex, highly nuanced feeling states that can dramatically change from moment to moment or hour to hour and can powerfully influence the choices we make.

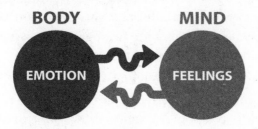

Figure 12.1   Emotions versus feelings.

While it's easy to think of emotions in discrete categories as good or bad, here's the headline:

All emotions, however nuanced, are important in decision-making!

In short, the essential goal for any of us is to become aware of our emotions and understand the unique way in which they present themselves to us, and in parallel becoming aware of how our *feelings* can be used to support wise decisions. For example, anger may reveal itself as a tight sensation in the chest; happiness may be felt through a sense of warmth and fullness in the heart area; disgust may be experienced as a tight pit in the stomach. This is how body-driven data presents itself, and without being able to recognize the signs and understand the underlying message, we have only a narrow aperture with which to make an informed judgment call.

Every emotion has a unique biochemical signature, which, after speedy neural processing to make personalized meaning, produces a distinct feeling state. Is it excitement or stress I feel? Anger or jealousy? Anxiety or curiosity?

Some emotions give rise to pleasant feelings, like joy, love, and fun. Other emotions elicit unpleasant feelings, like fear, anxiety, and insecurity. As stated earlier, all emotions, whether we think of them as good or bad, are a fundamental part of being human. The goal is not to feel joy, inspiration, and happiness 24/7, but rather to identify all our emotions and to manage the resulting feelings in a way that enhances our overall health and well-being. This means acquiring new knowledge, awareness, and language skills that contribute to the delicate process that enables wise and smart choices.

To wire sound decision-making processes into our integrated mind-body systems, it is helpful to distinguish between two basic categories of emotions: those that are perceived as pleasant and enjoyable and those that are perceived as unpleasant and unenjoyable.

We will call emotions that are pleasant and stir us to move forward, to advance, to seek more, and to grow "positive emotions." It is important to note that here we speak of *prosocial* emotions, those that are adaptive, socially acceptable, and typical in mentally well individuals. The other major category of emotions, those that are unpleasant and stir us to halt, to move backward, to retreat or to fight, are called "negative emotions." In addition to the positive and negative *valence* of emotions, described in the previous chapter, is the issue of *intensity*.

Some emotional responses produce feelings that are highly intense and powerful, and others are, by comparison, mild and subtle. Learning to differentiate (decode) emotions and their corresponding feeling states represents a critical step in acquiring emotional control, sometimes referred to as emotional literacy. In the context of this book, emotional control or emotional literacy represents the acquired ability to identify, comprehend, and moderate how the flow of emotion impacts human decision-making.

Emotions and the feelings they produce bring radiant color to our lives but also can unintentionally short-circuit our decision-making in tragic ways. Reflect for a moment on decisions you may have made when you were feeling jealous, exhausted, angry, resentful, or enraged. Even positive emotions such as excitement, enthusiasm, and optimism can derail our efforts to make wise decisions. Unbridled excitement for purchasing a home you can't afford, uncontrolled enthusiasm for the money you could make on a stock transaction, or ungrounded optimism for repaying a loan you should never have taken out in the first place can hijack our ability to make good, solid decisions.

THE OBJECTIVE IS NOT TO SILENCE EMOTION

It's important to understand that the goal for managing emotion in decision-making is neither to simply suppress unpleasant emotions nor to perpetually feel pleasant emotions. That's just not how real life works. Instead, the objective is to draw insight and understanding from whatever emotions and related feelings are bubbling up in the moment, listen to them, integrate the information with other relevant input, and discern both what is happening and how you feel about it. Then, using that information, you can more wisely choose either to act or not to act. The main point is that when you are able to properly decipher and integrate complex emotional data, you have a much better grasp of the full range of choices before you.

Antonio Damasio put it this way:

"Affect (emotion) is not just necessary for wisdom, it's irrevocably woven into the fabric of every decision."

Damasio's game-changing research revealed the powerful and dynamic nature of both how and why our emotions are indelibly integrated into our every thought, feeling, and decision. Information is entering our sensory system every nanosecond of life via chemical and electrochemical signals that pulse throughout our viscera, heart, lungs, gut, skin, and smooth muscles that are everywhere in our body.

Our five senses—sight, smell, sound, taste, and touch—can be thought of as "sensory portals" that constantly provide new input into the continuously updated personalized database, our Y.O.D.A.. Via our five primary senses, we absorb information, process it, and synthesize it to assist the brain in predicting what's coming next, thereby enabling it to make better, more informed decisions.

Wisdom Decision Insights: Our mind-body wisdom is distributed *throughout our bodies*. Engineered in a highly complex and coordinated manner, our fully integrated mind-body architecture captures data from geographically dispersed areas via our nervous system and, with proper training, can provide timely and relevant information critical to making wise and responsible decisions. This biologic concept of the mind as dispersed throughout the body provides a good sense for the basic underlying wiring of our emotions. Feelings are not simply an independent fabrication of our brains. They are the result of a cooperative partnership between the body and the brain, interacting by way of free-ranging chemical molecules and nerve pathways that result in our personalized perception of the world around us (like our own unique designer sunglasses with prescription lenses), created by the interaction between nature and nurture. The scientific truth is that our emotions undergird our feelings, and our feelings, for better and for worse, powerfully influence how we think, behave, and make choices.

It All Begins with Awareness

It should be clear now that wise decision-making requires, first and foremost, having an awareness not only of our emotions in the moment, but, equally important, of the messages being sent via feelings emanating from those emotions. Understanding what we are feeling at any particular time and the "why" behind those feelings represents priority one.

But how do we learn to gain an awareness of our feelings and emotions? How do we begin to understand the language in which they're communicating with us, and to give them names and identities so that we may use them wisely?

Neither home nor school typically offers codified instruction on the language of emotion, nor the ways in which both our minds and bodies create emotion. The Yale Center for Emotional Intelligence describes this awareness and skill set as being an "emotion scientist" (*Hmm. . .what's really happening here?*) rather than an "emotion judge" (*She shouldn't be upset right now. Her life is perfect!*).

As repeatedly emphasized, balancing insightful emotional data with sound rational intellectual information is the objective. One without the other can lead to disastrous decisions and choices. Both capacities must be artfully summoned and constantly practiced to achieve true proficiency. Every effort should be made both to acknowledge and to understand the feelings being sent by our emotional brain before important decisions are made. In other words, wise decision-making simply cannot be achieved in the absence of emotional intelligence.

RULER

Marc Brackett is the founding director of the Yale Center for Emotional Intelligence. In his book, *Permission to Feel*, he describes an evidence-based approach to social and emotional learning that has been implemented by over 3,500 pre-K to high schools throughout the U.S, with a study currently underway to adapt the highly successful program for early childhood settings. He and his colleagues at Yale have named the program RULER, an acronym for Recognize, Understand, Label, Express, and Regulate.

Unless your family is the rare exception, emotional intelligence was not a common topic at home. After examining multiple possibilities, Dr. Brackett decided that school, where all children are required to be present and engage during the foremost years of brain development, was the logical place to conduct a randomized controlled study on the impact of the RULER program on children.

The original goal of RULER was to help teachers and students learn a brand-new language, the mind-body lexicon of emotions. The program focused on building skills and knowledge in classroom settings to identify, understand, and manage emotions wisely, with the hypothesis that RULER would improve behavior, relationships, academic achievement, and mental wellness. Twenty years later, with dozens of peer-reviewed research papers published in prestigious scientific journals, this is precisely what the Yale team found.

By embedding emotion skills, language, and strategic practice into daily school life, teachers and students alike learned vital life skills that helped them feel better, perform at a higher level, and maintain healthier relationships.

Not only did RULER improve outcomes for individual students and wellness for teachers, it also had a tremendous impact on school culture and climate. And as we know from decades of social science research, the emotional climate of any physical space and those who come together within it, whether a home, school, office, or sports club, is one of the most impactful levers there is to foster a sense of belonging within a community of individuals. This sense of belonging, a major overarching theme across the social sciences (human beings need one another for health and survival), created the conditions in RULER schools that fueled the improved outcomes examined by the Yale research team.

The Takeaway: Healthy emotional climates drive health and sustainable performance, whereas unhealthy emotional climates do just the opposite.

The primary strengths of RULER are that it is practical, concrete, and research-based. Brackett contends that the more we can recognize, label, express, and, importantly, regulate our emotions, the better equipped we are to manage stressful situations in a thoughtful, proactive, and measured capacity.

As the RULER data and other emotion-focused scientific studies have shown in various contexts, including both home and work, emotion skills, when used properly, lead to better health, more adaptive and resilient behavior, improved relationships, higher levels of academic achievement and career success, and a self-reported sense of holistic well-being, all of which connect to making better choices.

As an interesting side note, after further research and study over several years, Salovey and Mayer expanded their definition of emotional intelligence to include the capacity to reason about emotions, to use the different states in an active and intentional manner to enhance thinking and judgment. The concept of using emotions to facilitate clear and well-informed thinking, of harnessing the related feeling states to augment rational thought, takes us to the *central core* of decision-making.

Wise Decision Insights for Managing Emotion

- Recruit your capacity for reflective consciousness and, before important decisions are made, answer the following questions for yourself:

    - What is my emotional brain saying to me about this decision?

- What is my current emotional state?

- What is my current energy state? Which quadrant am I in?

- Do the emotions I am currently feeling help or hurt my ability to make the right decision?

- Delay, postpone, or defer any important decision until the emotions you're feeling, both positive and negative, have cooled enough so as to not cloud your rational thinking ability. Put simply, avoid hot-minded decisions.

- Remember, the best decisions are made when you combine emotional insights with rational insights. Balancing these two valued sources of information enhances wise decision-making.

- Avoid making important decisions when you are tired, hungry, sleep-deprived, or needy. The human system is highly integrated. Your physical well-being, emotional well-being, mental well-being, and spiritual well-being are all connected and can powerfully influence the choices you make.

- To distance yourself from emotional biases that could cloud or distort decision-making, coach yourself from the third person. Coaching yourself from your own name can provide more distance and objectivity than "I" or "you" self-coaching.

- Use exercise and movement to reset your emotional state, thereby allowing more *constructive* emotional understandings and insights to surface.

- Meditation, deep breathing, and any activity that contributes to a meaningful emotional reset has real value in decision-making. Quieting the mind allows your capacity for reflective consciousness to assist in decoding emotional messages connected to an important decision.

- Use nature and sunlight to activate emotional insights prior to making important choices. A riverwalk, following a deeply wooded trail, or a stroll through a community park where you can look up at the sky, feel the air on your face, observe nature in full bloom, and see children laughing and playing

can suddenly produce important emotional clarity and understanding not easily achieved in indoor settings, such as at home
or in the office.

- Use humor to change a toxic internal chemistry that will likely
distort or undermine the choices you're about to make. Laugh
tapes, funny movies, hysterical podcasts, and the like can
change a dysfunctional mood within minutes.

- Use journaling to acknowledge, express, and discern your
emotions. Emotional literacy can be enhanced with regular
writing or printing.

- Intentionally changing how you think about something or
someone, your mindset, can trigger significant changes in how
you feel. When destructive emotions such as jealousy, envy, or
pride interfere with your decision-making, deliberately create
a different story in your mind. Different stories (still based in
fact) and different interpretations can lead to powerful shifts
in ongoing feelings and emotions.

- To increase your emotional literacy in decision-making, get
into the habit of labeling the emotions you are sensing, and
their corresponding outward-facing feeling states, at any
particular time. Do this in the kitchen while making dinner,
while out walking the dog, in conversation with friends. Practice, practice, practice, and myelinate those neural pathways
to create automatic habits. Once labeled, acknowledging and
discerning the prevailing emotions and their related feelings
becomes more accessible and provides actionable data.

- Check the following boxes before making an important
decision:

  ☐ Am I over- or underreacting emotionally regarding this
  decision?

  ☐ Have I fairly weighed the facts and feelings on both sides
  of the decision?

  ☐ Am I certain that the facts I'm working with that have produced the feelings I have are grounded in reality?

☐ Is this the right time to make this decision given my current feeling state?

☐ Am I hiding or concealing any important feelings from myself pertaining to this decision?

☐ Imagine what you will likely feel in three months regarding this decision.

☐ Imagine what you will likely feel in 1, 5, and 25 years regarding this decision.

A Few Final Things to Ponder

Human decision-making is highly complex and our emotional brains are always center stage in the decision-making process. For better or for worse, our physical, emotional, mental, spiritual, and even financial health are profoundly influenced by our day-to-day feelings and emotions. We all must become better emotional intelligence students to truly achieve wisdom in our decision-making.

Reflect for a moment on the big decisions you've made thus far in your life. How would you rate yourself? Is there a pattern that you can recognize in the decisions you now regret making? Were you too risky or to risk-averse in your choices? Were your bad decisions typically more impulsive, emotional, or irrational? Did you thoroughly vet the risk/reward consequences? Did you fully explore all other alternatives before deciding? Did you reject or follow any prevailing rules with your choice? Finally, did you examine the choices you had made through the lens of your deepest values and beliefs?

Using our capacity for reflective consciousness in managing our emotions represents an invaluable decision-making asset.

So much is at stake!

CHAPTER 13

The Inner Voice and Managing Stress

The story most of us tell ourselves around stress needs some serious updating because all of the statements listed below are capable of seriously compromising our ability to make wise and responsible decisions. Have any of these messages gotten through to your inner command center?

- Stress is harmful.

- Stress is to be avoided at all costs.

- Stress undermines your health and happiness.

- A happy and fulfilling life is a stress-free life.

- Stress undermines your immune system.

- An important goal in life is to reduce stress as much as possible.

The research world on stress has contributed a plethora of important new biological facts that Y.O.D.A. must incorporate into advising your inner voice regarding stress management and decision-making. Here are some important stress understandings that Y.O.D.A. can reference during the most challenging storms of our lives:

- The fact is that stress exposure is the stimulus for all growth in our lives. The hormones released during a stressful event are the hormones of life. Adrenaline, cortisol, DHEA, and the like prepare the body to respond to the stressor by increasing energy production, suppressing some biological functions, and stimulating brain growth. Without stress, all growth ceases.

- There is a culprit in the story of stress, however, and that culprit is *insufficient recovery*. Recovery is healing, restoration, and renewal. Without recovery, all stress eventually becomes excessive. Stress exposure stimulates growth, and recovery is when growth actually takes place in the human system.

- The real enemy is not stress but *chronic* stress, stress unabated by periodic recovery. The fitter and healthier you are physically, emotionally, mentally, and spiritually, the faster is your speed of recovery.

- The integrated mind-body system is basically an oscillatory system of synergistic, cascading energy pathways, a symphony of interwoven waves that are repeatedly evidenced in respiration, sleep, body temperature, appetite, menstruation, hormone levels, neurotransmitter levels, and the biophysiological machinery that generates energy for everyday activities, just to name a few. The rhythm of stress and recovery creates the pulse of life.

- In other words, no stress, no life; no recovery, no life.

- A critical insight regarding stress and decision-making is that protection from stress breeds weakness. When an arm or leg is in a cast due to a fractured bone, the healthy muscles that are completely protected from stress, because of the restriction of the cast, begin to atrophy almost immediately. This understanding applies not just to physical strength, but to emotional, mental, and spiritual (character) strength as well.

  - Once the cast is removed, the atrophied muscles must be progressively exposed to stress in order to regain full muscle functionality. This is what happens in physical therapy. Stress is certainly not the enemy here but rather the agent of renewal and growth.

- Everyone possesses limits on how much stress exposure can be constructively absorbed before damage is done. A fractured bone indicates the stress demand significantly exceeded the body's limits. The loss of a job, a failed marriage, or the death of a loved one can exceed our stress limits and, if not addressed, can lead to debilitating chronic stress, which is the real enemy.

- As has been pointed out in previous chapters, emotions provide important data, and if one uses their emotions wisely, even so-called negative emotions such as intense anger, fear, depression, panic, hopelessness, and anxiety can be viewed as a clear signal that you are approaching your stress limits and prioritizing recovery should be given immediate priority. If possible, important decisions should not be made during times of unrelenting, persistent stress.

- The word "stressful" can be used to describe an *event* or one's *response* to an event, such as anger or fear. A stressful response is typically thought of as uncomfortable or unpleasant. It's important to understand, however, that an event doesn't cause a response. Rather, it's our perception of the event, our internal story about what *is* happening, what *should be* happening, or what *has* happened that determines our response.

  - The very same event that is terrifying for one person can, for another individual, be thrilling, such as performing on stage in front of thousands of people. Because what's real in the mind is also real in the body at a biochemical level, creating adaptive, resilience-building stories out of any event, particularly when confronted by unavoidable hard things in life, protects our health, overall well-being, and ability to make sound decisions. More important than what happens to us in life is the story we create around what happens to us.

- When making important decisions, it's important to learn to discriminate between normal stress and excessive stress. What are the signs of excessive stress from your internal perspective?

What does it feel like? The more quickly and accurately you can recognize the signals, the more skilled you can become in making decisions during periods of high stress by strategically calling forth episodes of recovery prior to making the decision itself.

Stress and Narrowing of the Aperture

The psychological literature is rife with examples of what happens when we are under excessive stress. Our purview tends to narrow as we zoom in, hyper-focusing on the granular details of the problem, often amping up our anxiety in the process. Seeing only a sliver of the story, usually the bad part, too often results in a form of mental inflexibility and rigidity that can completely undermine our ability to make sound decisions. When stress levels are excessive and we fail to buffer the stress with sufficient recovery, we tend to fall back on old and well-trodden behavioral paths such as mindless snacking, binge-watching movies, or alcohol consumption. This happens because our narrow aperture simply doesn't allow any other viable alternative to rise to the surface.

Can you think of a situation in your own life, right now, in which, because of high stress, you find yourself using a narrow versus a wide aperture in your efforts to make the right decision? (See Figure 13.1.) Zooming in and then zooming out can help achieve new, breakthrough insights that dramatically expand the options you have in your decision-making equation.

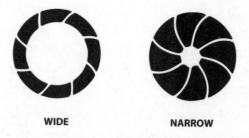

WIDE   NARROW

Figure 13.1   Decision-making needs to happen through both narrow and wide apertures.

STRESS BASICS FOR Y.O.D.A.

- The things that have pushed you the most in life can often become a source of enduring confidence, as long as they are well managed and you've given yourself the time and space to properly recover. An example is COVID-19. You are better prepared to handle another pandemic because of all you've suffered through and survived. Your capacity to handle the social, emotional, physical, and even financial effects of another pandemic have been greatly expanded because of the gut-wrenching stress exposure.

- The human body is always seeking balance. The sympathetic arm of our nervous system mobilizes the body for immediate action (fight, flight, or freeze) when faced with a stressful event, and the parasympathetic arm (rest and digest) initiates restoration, renewal, and healing.

  Both of these dynamic physiological systems can powerfully impact the choices we make. Are we in stress-recovery balance as we make this decision? Are we ramping up or shutting down, turning on or turning off, pushing forward or stepping back, investing or recovering? Based on our answers to such questions, when would be the optimal time to make this decision?

- Today's fast-paced, demanding world requires that we look for every opportunity possible to expand our capacity for good decisions under stress. The mindset that every storm of stress can be leveraged to grow our decision-making proficiency represents a game changer for nearly everyone. In a paradoxical way, every dose of stress can be considered a gift, one more opportunity to learn how to make extraordinary choices in difficult times.

- A helpful way of thinking about stress and recovery is to conceptualize stress as simply **energy expenditure** and recovery as **energy restoration and renewal**. Stress (energy expenditure) can be physical, emotional, mental, or spiritual, and so must recovery. Energy out must be balanced with energy in.

Balancing *physical* stress with recovery involves healthy nutritional input, hydration, exercise, strategic movement, sleep, and intermittent periods of rest.

Balancing *emotional* stress with recovery involves intentionally summoning positive emotions, such as joy, optimism, hope, love, gratitude, inspiration, and inner peace.

Balancing *mental* stress with recovery involves allowing the neurons that have been firing repeatedly to rest by focusing on something entirely different. Changing the focus and allowing the brain to take a deep breath allows for mental oscillation to occur.

Balancing *spiritual* stress with recovery involves reconnecting with your most cherished values, purpose in life, and core beliefs.

Energy expenditure (stress) not sufficiently balanced by energy renewal (recovery) leads to eventual burnout, disorder, and potential injury. Energy recovery not balanced with energy expenditure leads to atrophy and reduced capacity. Both of these forms of imbalance can seriously compromise our decision-making ability.

- *During particularly stressful times, stay connected to others.*

Human beings are, first and foremost, social creatures. Our ancestors survived by bonding together to face threats. Those who remained isolated and fought their battles alone found their odds of survival severely reduced.

Nature has equipped us with a powerful stress-combating hormone called oxytocin, sometimes known as the love hormone. It is produced by the posterior pituitary gland and inhibits the release of stress hormones like cortisol, thereby moderating fear and anxiety. Oxytocin is a primal ingredient in our recipe for survival, fueling the overwhelming feelings of love and connection a mother feels when she nurses her newborn baby.

Oxytocin also enhances emotional bonding and facilitates trust between individuals. Feeling compassion and love for others, experiencing gratitude and deep connection stimulates the release of oxytocin and can become a powerful perspective-balancing agent in decision-making.

* *Seek perspective in the storm.*

Best-selling author Richard Carlson, in his book *Don't Sweat the Small Stuff . . . and It's All Small Stuff,* argued that the little things that are essentially meaningless in the big picture can literally take over our lives.

What is needed when the storms of stress are fully raging is *perspective.* And sound decision-making without the right perspective is virtually impossible. Because of the profound way in which a shift in perception, seeing a situation through a new lens, can instantly change our view of the world, every effort should be made to seek the perspective that makes responsible, well-informed, and thoughtful decisions possible.

* *Take action on the things you can control and let the rest go.*

When you worry about things that are beyond your control, all you are doing is wasting precious energy.

What things can you control after a bad car accident, after your home is foreclosed upon, after a failed marriage? If chaos is everywhere, prior to any important decision, make the effort to create order somewhere. Make your bed, clean the house, wash your car, reach out to a friend, meditate, or go for a relaxing walk in nature.

Make a list of what you can control and what you cannot. Do something constructive that reduces chaos before making important choices. Continue taking positive steps, *in advance of important choices*, to make yourself and your situation right.

- *Time travel to get the priority right.*

    Prior to making your next big decision, when your stress levels are high, assess whether your angst and worry are truly necessary and appropriate by jumping ahead 3 months, 1 year, 5 years, or even 10 years to determine the real significance of the crisis you are facing. When looking forward through the lens of time, how important is it really? How will you reflect back on this at the end of your life? Was it worth the effort you put into it, or was it a complete waste of time and energy?

    So often, peering through the lens of extended time brings a much clearer sense of what's really at stake in the decision we are about to make. If an extraordinarily complex, potentially life-altering decision is front and center, viewing the situation from a distance can add valuable perspective that clarifies the risk-reward profile. One may discover that the consequences of a particular decision are simply too great to move on it or, conversely, that the short-term consequences pale in comparison to a choice that has strong potential to move emotional tectonic plates in the direction of True North.

CHAPTER **14**

The Role of Y.O.D.A. in Finding Flow

We've all been there before, immersed in a magical mind-body experience where we become so deeply absorbed in what we are doing that we literally become one with the activity. You become the ball in a tennis match, the notes in a piece of music, the puck in a hockey game, the brush while creating a painting, or the mountain you are scaling. There is only you and the act of doing.

"Flow" is a delicate psychophysiological state that facilitates performing to the upper limits of one's talent and skill. This concept of the special mind-body state was the brainchild of Mihaly Csikszentmihalyi, a brilliant professor of psychology at the University of Chicago who authored 14 books and over 200 research articles on the topic. In short, when awareness has merged so completely with whatever you are doing that they become inseparably fused together in space and time, you are in flow. Think Roger Federer playing a five-set match against Rafael Nadal—stunningly elegant masterful tennis! Second-guessing, self-doubting, negativity, and outcome fears are conspicuously absent, and so is self-consciousness and critical inner voice messages.

The questions to ask here are: How does the experience of flow and its supporting research connect to issues of personal wisdom and choice making? In what way does flow connect to one's inner voice and Y.O.D.A.? Of note, the flow state has been linked by researchers to issues of personal happiness, intrinsic motivation, accelerated learning, positive self-regard, engagement, emotional control, achievement in sports, student engagement, and a reduction in school crime.

Because of these and other potential benefits that can be derived from the experience of flow, equipping Y.O.D.A. with an understanding of how to access this special mind-body state could pay great dividends in setting the stage for wise decision-making throughout all dimensions of life.

Reflect on Your Flow Experience

The words people use to describe their own experience of flow are all remarkably similar. Here are just a few of the most common descriptors:

- Completely in sync with what I was doing
- An inner sense of complete calm and stillness
- Deeply absorbed in the activity, a total immersion
- Intensely focused in the moment
- I was not thinking; rather I was just doing
- Soothing sense of inner peace and quiet
- Felt as if someone else was doing it and I was just an observer
- Felt immersed in positive energy
- No fear, no doubts
- Felt like I was on autopilot
- Deeply satisfying and enjoyable
- Never wanted the experience to stop even though I was exhausted
- Felt completely alive and connected
- Confident I could reach the goal but it was okay if I didn't
- Had the feeling I was swimming in fun!
- The nervousness just vanished and I became completely free to just let go

Take a few moments and reflect on your own inner experience with flow. Describe what it feels like for you, in your own words, using the space provided.

MY FLOW EXPERIENCE

_____

_____

_____

_____

_____

For Y.O.D.A. to provide wise counsel to your inner coach (Inner Voice 2) regarding flow, understanding these concepts should prove helpful:

- Flow is more likely to occur when clear goals and objectives are established prior to the event.

- Flow is enhanced when the challenge being faced and the skills required to be successful are in relative balance. In other words, one can feel pushed beyond one's comfort zone but not pushed well beyond one's perceived level of competence.

- The more one focuses on the desired outcome during a performance, the less likely it is that flow will be experienced. The secret is to focus on the process of what one is doing, not the outcome.

- The more one can create a play frame around the event, a sense of deep joy in the doing, the more likely it is that flow will materialize.

- Accept the conditions one is facing "as is." Take whatever circumstances arise and move forward without hesitation. Never consider "Why on earth is this bad stuff happening to me?"

- Flow is more likely to occur when one can let go of the past or future and stay immersed in the present moment.

- Take in all the positives and let the negatives go.

- Do everything possible to keep one's ego out of it—absolutely no concern about what others think.

- The more one can take complete ownership for being there, for being intensely motivated to excel, the greater the probability of flow.

- Flow is more likely to occur when one remains positive, calm, cool, and collected, regardless of what's happening in the external environment.

- The more feelings of fun, enjoyment, joy, and love can be experienced simply in doing the activity itself, the greater the probability of flow.

- Following established spiritual, mental, emotional, and physical rituals and routines prior to the activity enhances the chances that flow will materialize.

INNER VOICE COACHING: MESSAGES TO ENHANCE FLOW

- When the conditions get rough:

    "You've *got* this!"

- When anger over mistakes starts to bubble up:

    "Focus on the present!"

    "There's only now!"

    "Focus on your breathing—deep inhale and deep exhale."

- When you're thinking too much:

    "Trust in yourself."

    "Stay with your process."

    "Be instinctive and automatic."

- When you are focusing too much on the mechanics and details:

   "Go with the flow."

   "Keep it simple."

   "Focus on the things you know you can do."

   "Stay immersed in the present."

- When you are getting uptight and tense:

   "You are great when the pressure is on."

   "Great opportunity to handle nerves better!"

   "Slow down and take your time."

- When you're performing poorly in a sport and not having fun because of it:

   "Find enjoyment in just trying to get better!"

   "Pat yourself on the back just for being out here!"

   "Find ways to learn and improve in spite of the situation."

   "Keep trying until you solve the riddle."

   "Never, ever give up! Hang in there!"

   "You love hard things and this is hard, so lean in!"

- When you feel out of it and discouraged:

   "Control what you can and let the rest go."

   "You have everything you need. You can get through this."

   "This is a great opportunity to strengthen your ability to bounce back, to be resilient. *Use* it!"

Wise Decision Insight: Because flow represents an exquisitely balanced mind-body state, it is an excellent time to ponder challenging decisions that must be made.

CHAPTER 15

Y.O.D.A. Guided Storytelling

Human beings are storytellers. This basic biosocial scientific fact is the simple reality of how our brains are wired, and the way oral history has been passed down from one generation to the next since the dawn of humankind. Stories represent our personal reality, just as this book is the authors' shared story about decision-making.

There are real stories, fake stories, tragic stories, life-changing stories, and harmful stories. Stories can be true, fabricated, pure fantasy, inspirational, grounded in facts, tainted with falsehoods, or completely authentic. Every time we speak to others or to ourselves we are storytelling, drawing upon our cognitive and physiological resources to construct and reconstruct narratives from various memories that are stored throughout our brain and body. Inner Voice 2 and Public Voice 2 are trained to send constructive and wise storytelling messages to our command center.

Great coaches are skillful, strategic, and effective storytellers. They understand the long-game goals and help us map our storytelling toward the outcomes that will serve us best in the end. They see and understand why taking the hard right over the easy wrong is essential, and help us keep a firm grip on the steering wheel of sound decisions.

THE TRUTH

As disturbing as it might be, we do not have direct contact with the real world. We only know the objective world indirectly through the filter of our senses, and our personalized experience of the events in our lives. The marvelous neuro-processor between our ears receives millions of bits of data every second streaming in through our senses—hearing, smell, sight, touch, and taste—and then we must make sense of the raw data. We do so by organizing it according to preexisting categories and meanings. The interpretation we give to the data forms a story (personal narrative) that becomes our story, our take on reality and, equally important, our reference point for decision-making.

The more our stories conform to the world as it actually exists, the better we can navigate life, find real solutions to the countless challenges we face every day, and make better choices. It is characteristically human to see the world the way we want to see it, rather than the way it actually is, and our choices and our grasp of right and wrong can be powerfully influenced by tainted input from faulty stories. When we fail to recognize that a piece of incoming data is faulty, the stories and beliefs and the decisions built upon that data will also be faulty. The stories we form in life, even those we consider *foundational*, perhaps even *sacred*, can be contaminated by biased data and faulty interpretation.

Research has identified no less than 25 ways our neuro-processing system can compromise our storytelling and sound choices. Several examples were detailed in the introduction of this book, including motivated reasoning and confirmation bias. Others include conformity dynamics, rationalization, obedience to authority, social approval, cultural forces, and strong emotion.

It's important to acknowledge that our beliefs are simply opinions (interpretations) that we accept as true but may or may not be grounded in reality. Unfortunately, our beliefs often masquerade as fact-based truth and are, therefore, accepted without thoughtful scrutiny. When we lose touch with the world as it actually exists, the tragic cost is the lost battle for truth in our stories and the decisions that flow from those stories.

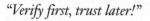

"Verify first, trust later!"
—Russian Proverb

Y.O.D.A.'s KEYS FOR STORYTELLING AND DECISION-MAKING

Key 1: Ground your stories and your decisions in fact-based truth.

Pyrite is a shiny yellow iron-based mineral that appears much like pure gold. Referred to as fool's gold, pyrite—which has virtually no real market value—has duped countless prospectors for decades into believing they have struck it rich. Before doing the essential mineral assay verifying the truth, some foolishly began celebrating, spending money, and doing everything millionaires do. Pyrite is, metaphorically speaking, *fake truth*.

It may be what we want to believe, hear, or see, but it's not the real deal—it's fake! In the context of this book, gold is fact-based truth and we must be lifelong prospectors in search of it. Because of our propensity for self-deception, we can be fooled by fake truth (pyrite) and, unfortunately, pyrite is everywhere. Social media is awash in pyrite. News outlets of all shapes and sizes are in the business of selling pyrite, and they do it because people buy it and it supports their agenda.

Getting to the truth when surrounded everywhere by "fool's gold" is hard, exhausting work and, after all the effort we make to get to the truth, what we find may not be what we had hoped for. The results of what we discover may be painful and disappointing, but as prospectors of reality-based truth, we got what we were searching for: the truth. And truth is always *pure gold* in our storytelling and decision-making.

SOME HUMOR

Pyritis (Fool's Gold): A brain disorder that distorts the truth, our storytelling, and our decisions.
Stage 1 Pyritis: Distortions in the truth and our storytelling exist but are relatively minor and inconsequential relative to our decision-making.

Stage 2 Pyritis: Distortions in the truth and storytelling are increasingly evident and some have significant negative consequences in the decisions we make.

Stage 3 Pyritis: Distortions in the truth and storytelling are frequent and pervasive, seriously eroding our decision-making process.

Stage 4 Pyritis: The line between fantasy and truth no longer exists. The decisions we make contain fatal flaws that seriously compromise the choices we make.

Ponder these questions:

- What if you can't trust your grocer's story of selling you uncontaminated food?

- What if you can't trust your utility company's story to provide power to your home?

- What if you can't trust the story your banker tells you about securely protecting your money?

- What if you can't trust the story your local police tell you that they will protect you?

- What if you can't trust the story your physician tells you about your health?

Statements that reflect wisdom in your storytelling and decision-making:

- "Here's the decision I should make based on what I know now."

- "I've learned to keep an open mind on most everything. I've learned from experience that I can get things very wrong in my head. I love to think I've got the most accurate perspective on things, but experience has taught me that's not always the case."

- "I must hold most everything tentatively and keep pushing the envelope for more truth."

- "There is the real world and then there is the world as I see it. I've learned the hard way that I must be open to constant adjustments in my thinking to get decisions right."

- "The reality I see is too often distorted by what I want to see. It's very disconcerting to confront how off I frequently am."

- "I wonder how much I know is, in reality, mostly fantasy."

- "When I ask myself what things I know for certain, I realize that in many cases they are nothing more than my beliefs. They are not actually grounded in verifiable facts."

- "Recognizing that my view of things must always be held as tentative is quite unsettling. I love being certain I'm right."

- "I'm asking my brain not to dupe me, not to create fantasy, so I feel better in the moment and make the easy choice. I want to see the world the way it really is, no matter how painful it is for me. I will take it from there."

Without truth, our storytelling and decision-making descends into chaos and disorder almost immediately. And this understanding applies to the decisions we make for ourselves, as well as those we make on behalf of others.

It's interesting that the first three letters in the word "truth" are the same first letters in the word trust: TRU. Simply put, truth builds trust in our storytelling and decisions.

"Memory is a curious machine and strangely capricious."
—Mark Twain

Key 2: Don't judge or make decisions until you have an unbiased story grounded in verifiable facts.

The U.S. justice system consists of courts, prosecutors and defense lawyers, judges and jurists. This machinery of justice has been carefully designed by the United States justice system to get to the truth about what happened or didn't happen. Without the ability to separate the facts of a case from fiction, the guilt or innocence of a person cannot be justly determined. The final decision of guilt or innocence is typically made by what is supposed to be an open-minded, unbiased third party. That third party may be a judge, a panel of judges, or a jury of unbiased citizens.

The challenge for all of us is that we must, in effect, hold court multiple times every day when we make critical decisions. We must ensure that before important decisions are made, we have authenticated the facts that we are using in our deliberation, we've tagged potentially corrupted, biased, and tainted files, and we've faced the truth about our own biases and personal desires.

When we hold court in our own minds, we are the court—the entire court! We must present the evidence fairly and courageously cross-examine ourselves to decide what data must be thrown out because it is contaminated. We simply must do everything we can to get as close to the 360-degree dataset to arrive at the truth, so we can get the decision right.

Key 3: Always convey to yourself that the facts you are considering could be wrong and, therefore, the decision you are making could be wrong.

Making a difficult decision should always be delivered within the context of humility and, with the understanding that (1) this is how you currently see it, and (2) you could be wrong. It's also important to immediately make corrections, if possible, when you get it wrong, and then firmly commit to learning from your faulty decision. Vow to get better every day.

Examples

"Here is how I have come to see it. First, it's important for you to understand that I've decided to tell you this solely out of my concern for you. Yes, I might be wrong, but I don't think so. John is not a good friend for you. He is always taking advantage of you. He uses you to get what he wants. I don't believe he is a friend you can trust and I'm worried for you."

"I've been wrong before but I strongly believe your decision to skip college is the wrong one. I only want the best for you. I don't have a crystal ball into your future but I fear this decision is not what's best for you in the long run. I want to talk further about this."

Key 4: Always deliver potentially painful decisions (your truth) within an emotionally supportive and caring climate. This applies to decisions that are tough on you as well as decisions that are tough on others.

Some decisions you make can be extremely painful and even debilitating for others, triggering almost instantaneous anger and defensiveness. Painful decisions require that your decision be delivered with compassion and warmth.

Examples

A compassionate decision from your boss to you:

"The company has decided to eliminate your position. This is the result of a downsizing directive that must occur or the company cannot survive. Please understand this action has nothing to do with your performance on the team. I consider you to be one of my best direct reports and I am deeply disturbed that I will be losing you."

Constructive story to yourself:

"Okay, you just lost your job and over 300 people at your firm have lost theirs as well. You have a six-month severance package and a great recommendation from your boss. You will get through this. You've done a great job here and you will find another place to showcase your talents."

Key 5: Make certain the story you are telling can take you where you want to go. So many messages we deliver to ourselves or others represent dead ends. One simply can't get to the intended destination with the story being told.

Examples

This story a tennis player tells herself won't get her where she wants to go:

"My forehand always fails me. I could have been a great player were it not for my damn forehand!"

This story does work for her:

"My forehand is holding me back now but with effort and dedication, it will one day be my best shot! I'm making the decision to work harder than ever to get the forehand I want. I know I have it in me!"

Deadend story:

"I'll never find someone like her again. She was the love of my life and I'm resigned to the fact that the best part of my life is over."

This story works with what he really desires:

"Now I know what I really want for my partner in life. I am deeply saddened that it won't be her, but I know I will find another with her amazing qualities. My decision is to keep looking."

Key 6: Align your story and the resulting decision with your core purpose for living, core values, and Best Self.

Ask yourself these questions:

Does the story I tell and the decision I'm about to make really represent me at my very best? Does my story and decision align with my core purpose in life (e.g. to be a positive force for good in the world)? Is there any part of my decision that is not consistent with what matters most to me?

Key 7: Make certain your story inspires hope and motivates you to take action.

Great stories move us, motivate us, and inspire us to go forward in life and make bold, constructive decisions. Recall a time when the story you told yourself or a story that was told to you had a powerful impact on your future, one that led to a significant breakthrough decision. Reflect on the elements of that story. What was it about the message that enabled you to make the courageous, right decision?

USING Y.O.D.A. TO MANAGE INTRACTABLE POLITICAL STORIES

Just as entire countries can become deeply divided over political differences, so can families, friends, relatives, and even business partners. The issue is that our political beliefs and our stories about what's morally right and wrong are inseparably bound together. Some issues can trigger smoldering hot emotions immediately. Place a check alongside any of the political issues listed here that represent volatile hot buttons for you:

_____ Abortion	_____ Socialism
_____ Climate change	_____ Voter fraud
_____ Immigration	_____ Fake news
_____ Gun control	_____ Free speech
_____ Critical race theory	_____ LGBTQ
_____ Death penalty	_____ Vaccines

Now, reflecting on issues you just checked, consider these questions from the perspective of your Best Decision-Making Self:

- How do you know your position is right, that your story on this issue is not tainted by false data?

- How much time have you spent looking at all the facts supporting the opposite side of the issue?

- How did your story on the issue get formed? Who or what influenced you the most?

- Is your story more fact-based or intuitively based?

- Would you bet your life or the life of a family member that you have your story right on the issue?

- Can you tolerate having an open discussion about the issue with those who have an opposing story? How defensive are you when your story gets challenged?

- Can you connect any of your own personal needs or wants with the story you have on the issue?

- Would you like those supporting the opposing political side to be silenced?

- Would you be willing to go to war or commit violent acts of civil disobedience to resolve the issue in your favor?

- Would you support any compromise on the issue?

- How likely are you to ever change your story on the issue, even when confronted with verifiable, contradictory evidence?

After considering these questions, is there any room for making adjustments to your story on these issues? In all probability, the stories you have told yourself regarding these issues have been granted full, unrestricted access to your inner command center, and will undoubtedly influence countless decisions you will make in the future, for better or worse.

It's critical that we remain open to new, relevant data, both contradictory and supportive, relating to our hot-button political stories. Because of the damage that faulty political stories can have on the operation of our decision-making machinery, we must always be open to adjustments and amendments to ensure we get it right.

All of the political issues listed above are extremely complex. There are no simple, one-dimensional answers. Real solutions are most often highly nuanced, reflecting important concessions on both sides of the argument. Extreme, rigid positions reveal more about *you* than about the issue itself.

Y.O.D.A.'s STORYTELLING KEYS FOR MANAGING POLITICAL CONFLICT

1. Whenever someone begins to discuss political views, summon your inner Y.O.D.A. immediately! Sit back and listen respectfully. When asked about your political positions, begin with something like: "It's complicated for me. I want to understand your positions and I'll do my best to communicate mine. I'm hoping there is some overlap."

2. When there are stark differences: "I respect your position and I hope you respect mine. I'm not sure I have the issue exactly right. I'm a work in progress and will always be open to rethinking my positions."

3. When there are stark differences among family members: "I want you to understand that no matter what your political views are, you will always have my respect and unconditional love. No political position you have will ever change that."

4. When people are tired, frustrated, angry, or stressed, refuse to discuss political differences: "With all due respect, let's pick up this conversation another time."

5. When irreconcilable differences come up: "Let's agree to disagree and move on. I respect your views and certainly understand how important they are to you. I value you far more than your politics. I hope you don't judge me too harshly for not agreeing with you. Perhaps someday we both will see things differently. I treasure our friendship."

PART IV

Y.O.D.A. TRAINING STRATEGIES

CHAPTER 16

Voice Training 101

Let's start with this:

The only path to self-directed change is through the door of reflective consciousness.

Humanity's greatest asset is its capacity for the kind of deep reflective consciousness that gives rise to personal transformation. It is the capacity to be aware that one is aware, to be conscious of what one is thinking or saying both privately and publicly, to be fully conscious of one's own awareness. Reflective consciousness is the essential difference that separates humans from all other species.

THE EVOLUTIONARY UPGRADE WITH NO EQUAL

Reflective consciousness is truly nature's evolutionary masterpiece. Without it, our future would be determined solely by the interaction of our environment and our genetic makeup. The mechanisms by which nature transformed simple consciousness into reflective consciousness is a profound neurobiological mystery. Put another way, how nature transformed three pounds of neurons and brain tissue into the human capacity for self-awareness and reflective consciousness is beyond our current understanding. Little by little, however, the scientific community is beginning to unravel this remarkable genetic mystery.

All species in the animal kingdom, including humans, possess the capacity for awareness. A deer or bear in the forest possesses a keen awareness of its environment. Any unusual sound, smell, or movement mobilizes the animal for immediate action to enhance survival. All animals, as well as humans, can be conscious or unconscious, aware or unaware, but only humans possess the capacity for reflective consciousness, the ability to observe consciousness itself. That precise, uniquely human capacity, was summoned when you were asked to answer the questions presented in Chapter 4, "Time for Serious Reflection."

Critical Understanding: Voice Training 101 begins with *reflective consciousness*.

Using Your Capacity for Reflective Consciousness, Ponder These Questions Before Making Important Decisions

- What is the central issue in the decision I am about to make?

- What do I really want as the long-term outcome here?

- What are other alternative choices that I should consider?

- What are the real consequences if I don't get this right?

- What are the risks on both sides?

- What am I not completely certain about relative to this decision?

- What are the trade-offs on both sides of the decision?

- What core values must I consider in making this decision?

- What are the likely long-term consequences of the decision I am about to make?

- What are the chances that my brain is being hijacked in making this decision? Am I deluding myself to get the decision I want?

- What does my Y.O.D.A. say is the right decision?

From "What" to "Who"

- Who are your closest family members you can trust in helping you make the right decisions in life?

- Who are the people you respect most for their ability to make well-informed, responsible decisions in good and bad times?

- Who has consistently given you sound advice in making the right choices over time?

- Who has gained your highest respect for choosing the *hard right* over the *easy wrong* in challenging moments?

- Who would you give unconditional access to your central command center because you have total trust that they always have your long-term best interests in mind?

- Who are three to five trusted people you would put on your **decision-making advisory board** whose counsel you would seek in making big life choices?

- _____

- _____

- _____

- _____

- _____

EIGHT-STEP TRAINING PROGRAM

Step 1: Purchase a journal and a small notebook that can fit into your back pocket (like golfers carry) or anywhere else you can access it quickly.

Step 2: For two weeks, become consciously aware of the tone and content of both your inner self-coaching voice and your public voice. Pay particular attention to your inner voice. Record in your small notebook how you speak to yourself, both "you talk" and "I talk" (e.g. "You're doing okay; you're an idiot; I can't believe I said that; I'm so unlucky"). Record as much "you talk" and "I talk" in your notebook as possible throughout the day. At the end of each day, transfer the messages from your notebook into your journal. Date every day's entry. This step is not complete until you have completed 14 days of recording your inner voice and public voice coaching messages. Each day's entries simply represent a sampling of that day.

Step 3: Review all 14 days of your notes and prepare a written summary of your findings in your journal. Things to consider in your summary: What kind of coach are you to yourself? Would you ever say the things you say to yourself to someone you deeply cared about? Are you pleased or shocked by what you learned in the two weeks of reflecting on your own self-coaching messages? Is your self-coaching predominantly positive and constructive or negative and hurtful? Does what you say to yourself breed self-confidence, health, and happiness or does it tend to undermine them? Would you be embarrassed if the coaching messages you gave to yourself were made public?

Step 4: Make a conscious decision to either (1) train to improve the tone and content of your self-coaching, or (2) leave as is. If you elect to train, proceed to step 5.

Step 5: Commit to journaling for a minimum of 5 to 10 minutes daily for a period of at least three months. One of the most effective ways of retraining the way your private and public voices speak to you is through handwriting. You simply script in advance the inner messages you would like delivered by your Y.O.D.A. in situations that have historically produced toxic or potentially harmful self-coaching. Examples could include:

> Traffic, competition, managing mistakes, misbehaving children, spouse's verbal attacks, disengaged employees, financial pressure, low energy, failure to meet expectations, politics, disrespectful children, choking in sports.

> For getting the scripts right, tap into your Best Self and Inner Y.O.D.A. Your Y.O.D.A. should be preloaded with your core purpose for living, your core values, your personal credo, and your ultimate mission in life.

Step 6: Most phones today have the ability to record voice memos. Simply go to your app store and select an app with voice memo recording capability. This enables you to coach yourself with your own public voice (you coaching yourself publicly).

Again, tap into your Best Self and Inner Y.O.D.A. to determine the best possible coaching script. Listening to you coaching yourself in your own voice can be a very powerful strategy for getting through to your inner command center.

Voice memos can also be very effective in embedding critical operating instructions into your command center, such as core purpose in life, core values and beliefs, and personal credo.

Step 7: Record all your training inputs daily in your journal. Training inputs are any intentional energy investment made in a given day to move raw Inner Voice 1 to trained Inner Voice 2 or raw Public Voice 1 to trained Public Voice 2. As we learned in Chapter 2, Inner Voice 1 and Public Voice 1 are untrained (potentially toxic) and Inner Voice 2 and Public Voice 2 are trained (constructive) coaching messages. The process of tracking your training activities is called "quantification" in the research world. Quantifying your training investments represents an important step in achieving the outcome you want.

Step 8: Say "stop" as soon as you become aware of any non-constructive self-coaching messages, either private or public. Immediately replace the faulty self-coaching with something helpful and constructive.

Another example: Immediately put your index finger over your lips signaling "Be quiet! Change the message now!"

Final recommendation: Stay with your voice training for at least 90 days. New habits require dedicated time and energy investment if they are going to truly last. The payoff is priceless!

CHAPTER 17

Using Y.O.D.A. to Get Home

May you live long enough to know why you were born.
—Cherokee Birth Blessing

You've been traveling by car for nearly two weeks on a family vacation. You've covered nearly 3,000 miles and now you're ready to return home. Your current location is very unfamiliar to you and you're not sure of the best route home. Immediately you reach forward and activate the car's navigation system.

A question appears on your screen: "What is your intended destination?" You respond "Home." But if your home address has not been preloaded into the system, the next prompt is: "What is the address?" Because you've recently moved to a new home, your car does not have the exact address in its system. You know the city, the suburb, and the street you live on, but the specific address completely slips your mind.

After several failed attempts to upload the adequate number of relevant details into your navigational system, you finally realize that without an exact address, your system cannot be relied on to get you home. *You must provide an exact address!*

For your car's navigation system to function properly, two coordinates are required: your exact current location and your exact intended destination. Without both data points precisely uploaded, the car's navigation system simply cannot be trusted to take you where you want to go.

THE TOMBSTONE EXERCISE

As defined here, home is your **ultimate destination** in life. It is the place where you want to end up when your life is over. For Y.O.D.A. to get you there, it must be provided with the precise coordinates to chart an accurate and efficient course. Countless decisions will be required between where you are now and where you want to end up, all of which will depend on the accuracy of the given coordinates. The following exercise is designed to help you determine where home is for you.

Determining Where Your "Home" Is

We call this the Tombstone Exercise. Set aside at least 30 minutes of quiet, uninterrupted time for reflection. Consider what you would most want inscribed on your tombstone to reflect who you actually were when you were alive. The words carved in stone should represent your highest priorities in determining what a truly successful life means to you. You may choose six to eight separate words, or alternatively a couple of short sentences.

In your soulful deliberation, consider society's scorecard for success in life, such as wealth, fame, achievement, privilege, and so on. Do you want any of these carved into your tombstone?

Now think about being a loving father, mother, son, or daughter. Consider any moral or ethical character strengths like integrity, kindness, loyalty, humility, compassion, caring, gratefulness, and generosity.

Figure 17.1   Consider the words you'd want on your tombstone.

Here's the critical understanding: *The words you finally choose to most accurately reflect how you want to be remembered in life is **home** for you.*

Whether this is your first or your tenth attempt to get this life coordinate right, you must continue to check the accuracy and overarching precision of what you have determined to be home for you. Getting this right is vital because it will become the filter through which all of your critical decisions and choices in life are made. And just as your car's navigation system requires a precise address, so does your Y.O.D.A. Once determined, "getting home" will be the single most important set of operating instructions to be programmed into your inner command center.

It's interesting that, after we are finally put to rest, the words that appear on our tombstone typically are chosen by others—and may or may not reflect who we really were in life. Words like selfish, arrogant, dishonest, or unfaithful are never inscribed. The unwritten but universally followed convention is to chisel something positive, whether true or not, or chisel nothing at all. By conscientiously completing this exercise, you get to decide, in advance, the impact you intend to leave behind. Now, and most importantly, you must live your life accordingly!

After careful and thoughtful reflection, write what getting home means to you:

_____

_____

_____

_____

_____

Establishing the Precise Address

The next step is to determine the precise address. This again requires soulful thought and serious reflection. To help you with this process, several examples are provided.

EXAMPLE 1

Step 1 in Getting Home: City and Zip Code

The words that appear on your tombstone are analogous to the city and zip code where your home is located.

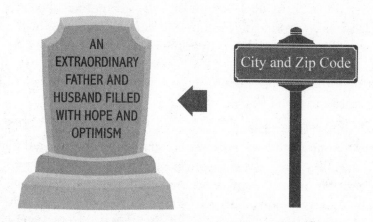

Figure 17.2   Choosing the words in the Tombstone Exercise is just the beginning in the process of getting home.

Step 2 in Getting Home: Precise Address

To determine the specifics, answer these questions:

1. What do you mean by "extraordinary father"? Be as specific and concrete as possible. Provide the criteria you must meet to arrive at that exact destination.

2. What do you mean by "extraordinary husband"? Be as precise and concrete as possible. To truly qualify as an extraordinary husband, what must happen, who must you be, how must you show up?

3. Explain what you mean by "filled with hope." How must you demonstrate this in the reality of your life on a daily or weekly basis? Give specific examples.

4. Explain what you mean by "filled with optimism." How does optimism become the legacy you wish to leave behind? Give concrete examples from the reality of your life.

PRECISE ADDRESS

Figure 17.3

EXAMPLE 2

Step 1 in Getting Home: City and Zip Code

Here is another example of "getting home."

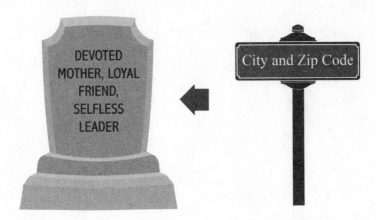

Figure 17.4

Step 2 in Getting Home: Precise Address

To determine the specifics, answer these questions:

1. What do you mean by "devoted mother"? How do you qual-
    ify at the highest level? What does "devoted" mean? Provide
    everyday examples.

2. What do you mean by "loyal friend"? Describe in as much
    detail as possible what that means to you. What must happen
    in the reality of your life for this to be the truth?

3. Explain as precisely and thoughtfully as possible what being a "selfless leader" means to you. How do you qualify? How must you show up? How does this legacy become reality?

PRECISE
ADDRESS

Figure 17.5

EXAMPLE 3

Step 1 in Getting Home: City and Zip Code

Here is a third example of "getting home."

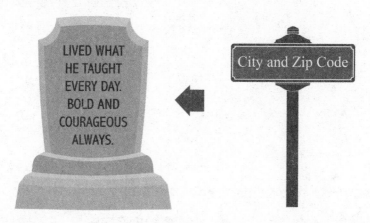

Figure 17.6

Step 2 in Getting Home: Precise Address

To determine the specifics, answer these questions:

1. Explain what you must do to qualify as a person who "lived what he taught every day." Be as specific and concrete as possible and provide some real-life examples.

2. What does "bold" mean in the reality of your life? How do you manifest it on a daily basis? What must happen for this to become your lasting legacy?

3. What does "courageous" mean to you? What must you do in the reality of your life to qualify? Be as precise and specific as possible.

PRECISE ADDRESS

Figure 17.7

EXAMPLE 4

Step 1 in Getting Home: City and Zip Code

Here is a final example of "getting home."

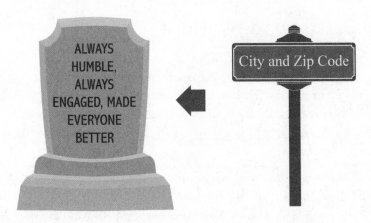

Figure 17.8

Step 2 in Getting Home: Precise Address

To determine the specifics, answer these questions:

1. Explain what "always humble" means in the reality of your life. Give concrete and precise examples.

2. How do you qualify in life for being "always engaged"? Provide real-life examples of how you must show up in the here and now in order to do this.

3. How do you "make everyone better" in the reality of your life? What specific behaviors must you constantly engage in and model for others to achieve this goal?

PRECISE
ADDRESS

Figure 17.9

THE OBSESSION TO GET HOME

In Chapter 11, "Managing Energy and Your Inner Voice," you learned how the investment of energy spawns growth. Extraordinary growth requires extraordinary investment. No one wants their legacy in life to be "just average," ordinary mother, father, friend, leader, and so on. No one wants their legacy to be garden-variety courage, honesty, integrity, kindness, or goodness.

In other words, if getting home represents the crescendo of your life and the ultimate purpose for being alive, nothing but extraordinary should be acceptable. This means constant and continuous investment of your full and best energy week after week, year after year, for what-ever time you have left on planet earth. It must become

Your magnificent obsession

None of the things carved on your tombstone can be gifted, bor-rowed, leased, or inherited. You must create them and live them. You take life from your body and literally make them come to life in the reality of who you really are, day after day after day.

City, Zip Code, and Address for Your Home

You're now ready to establish the exact location of home for you. It's a two-step process.

Step 1 in Getting Home: Your City and Zip Code

Inscribe the words that best represent your **ultimate destination** at the end of your life. These words are the ones you would use to define a truly successful life for you.

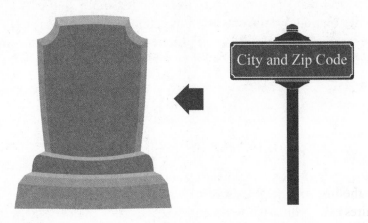

Figure 17.10

_____

_____

_____

_____

_____

Step 2 in Getting Home: Your Precise Address

Describe in specific detail what you must do to make these words or sentences become the reality of how you will be remembered when you are gone:

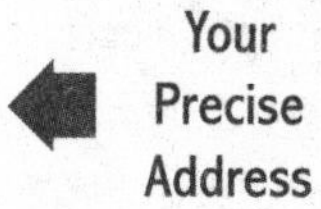

_____

_____   ◀   Your Precise Address

_____

_____   **Figure 17.11**

Wise Decision Insight: The journey *toward* home is what transforms us.

It's important to understand that we never completely reach our precise address. We simply get closer, better, more aligned with our final destination. It's the obsession to get home that transforms us, day after day, year after year. Getting home is our North Star for a truly successful life.

CHAPTER 18

Summary Wisdom from Y.O.D.A.

Consider both of the following scenarios, which demonstrate how challenging and difficult everyday decisions can be.

SCENARIO **1**

You are an elite competitive athlete. You have been training since you were seven years old to be the best in the world in your sport. You've sacrificed everything, but it's not looking like your athletic dreams, which have become nearly an obsession with you, will ever become reality. A close friend of the family happens to be a brilliant molecular scientist and he presents you with an intriguing proposition. According to him, he has broken the biochemical code for achieving nearly unlimited athletic success. Here were his points:

- All your athletic dreams will come true. You will never lose again.

- All you have to do is take a pill and the competitive world of sports will be yours. It is important for you to know, however, that the ingredients contained in the pill are banned and taking the pill represents a form of cheating.

- Because the pill represents an unprecedented breakthrough in science, your scientist friend is 100% certain that it will not be detected in any drug testing now or ever in the future.

- Yes, all of your athletic dreams will come true, but there is one serious downside: You will die from taking the pill in five years.

So, before making your decision, let's get both sides of the decision completely clear. **Decision 1** is to take the pill and have all your athletic dreams come true, knowing full well it's clearly cheating but you will never get caught, and you will die in five years from taking the pill. **Decision 2** is not to take the pill, knowing full well your athletic dreams will likely never materialize.

I know, you're probably thinking this is completely absurd. No one in their right mind would choose **Decision 1**. But hold on a minute. This same proposition was presented to elite athletes in an anonymous questionnaire every year for nearly a decade. The results will shock you. Referred to as the "Goldman Dilemma," the survey was given to nearly 200 high-level athletes annually, and roughly half responded that they would take the pill.

So the obvious question is: How could any rational person make such a bad decision? What convoluted logic and twisted thinking could account for why so many athletes would make such a disastrous choice? Decisions like this—and we have all made them at some point in our lives—underscore how flawed and fragile the human decision-making process really is. The lure of extrinsic achievement, of fame, money, notoriety, and recognition, is capable of completely hijacking our ability to make sound choices in life.

Scenario 2

For as long as you can remember, you have been inspired by everyday people who have made a significant contribution to the betterment of mankind, people like Martin Luther King, Mahatma Gandhi, Mother Teresa, and Mother Cabrini. Because of people like them and the example of service to others they have set for everyone, you have decided to pursue a career in politics to do exactly that. You are intelligent, informed, an outstanding speaker, passionate, and a person of high integrity. You are driven to improve people's lives.

After nearly two decades of hard, demanding work, you finally get elected to Congress. Words cannot begin to express how excited and appreciative you are for this opportunity to contribute. You have a clear set of priorities and action items that represent the central core of your promises to the constituents who elected you.

Almost immediately after arriving in Washington, all freshman members of Congress are called to a mandatory meeting of their political party. The message was clear and ominous: If you want to be around for more than one term, you must follow the dictates of your party, with no exceptions, whether or not you agree with the decisions or policies. "Play ball or you won't be around to play ball in your second term. Period!" The party leader running the session went on to say that in just two to three terms, you will become very successful financially, will possess considerable power, and will be recognized as a political leader on the world stage.

So let's examine the choices you have in this situation. **Decision 1** is that you agree to faithfully follow your party's dictates in casting votes, in supporting your party's policies, and in aligning all your public speaking with the party's priorities. In doing so, you must unfortunately walk away from many of the promises you made to those who elected you. This decision will clearly compromise your integrity but will certainly provide real financial security for your family, something you are deeply concerned about.

Decision 2 is not to adhere robotically to your party's mandates and to accept whatever political consequences there might be from your decision, even if it means you will have no second term. You are committed to following your own judgment in all matters, with the highest consideration honoring the promises made to those who elected you. Choosing this option will likely result in your being in Congress for only one term and will involve real financial challenges for your family.

Now, considering both sides as presented, make your decision. Again, you might immediately choose **Decision 2** because it's obviously the right thing to do. However, the reality of how freshmen in Congress make this choice is all too familiar to anyone who's watching. Being called Congressman or Congresswoman is so intoxicating, the financial upside so alluring, the personal power so appealing, the brain can only see **Decision 1** as a viable option. And this will all occur below our conscious radar, so there will be no feelings of guilt, no compromised sense of integrity, no loss of honor.

Both scenarios 1 and 2 demonstrate how frail and unreliable our decision-making machinery actually is. If any hope exists in shoring up the flawed system, it is in confronting the system's weaknesses and doing the heavy lifting every day to repair it. Remember, our uniquely human superpower is our capacity for reflective consciousness, and it is only in leveraging this remarkable human asset that the system can be righted.

To summarize, **Wise Decision Insights** can help repair the system that determines so much of our destiny in life:

- Because health ignites wisdom in decision-making, strive to establish daily habits that steadily improve your physical, emotional, mental, and spiritual health. Identify concrete practices that will strengthen your literacy in all four areas of interrelated health, because these represent the bedrock of sound, time-tested decision-making.

- Strengthen your capacity for reflective consciousness every day of your life. The brain's ability to observe itself, to listen to its own inner voice, to witness itself intentionally distorting reality to achieve some end represents our only real hope for controlling our destiny. This is our true superpower.

- Understand that your perceptions of the world around you are simply interpretations, nothing more. The truth that you see is inherently subjective. Make every effort to align your view of the world with your deepest values and core purpose for living and never tire in your efforts to find and embrace objective truth.

- Assume most incoming data is partially or completely flawed in some way. Quarantine all data that poses a genuine risk of compromising your decision-making process. Protect your inner core at all costs.

- Consciously decide who should and who shouldn't be granted full access to your inner core, the sacred processing center for all of the important decisions you make.

- For five days, record as accurately as possible the tone and content of your inner voice. When completed, answer the following question: What kind of advisor/coach are you to yourself?

- Estimate how many decisions you make in a single hour, from small things, like what you will eat for breakfast, to large things, like whether you should have the difficult conversation with your spouse today. From your one-hour sample, estimate how many decisions you make in a month. Next, answer the following question: What are you referencing when you make decisions, particularly important ones?

- Consciously vet future important decisions you make through the following seven lenses:

  - Best Self

  - Best Moral Self

  - Primary Life Purpose

  - Tombstone Legacy

  - Core Values and Beliefs

  - Personal Credo

  - Ultimate Mission in Life

- Instantly summon Y.O.D.A. when important decisions are called for. Whenever possible, intentionally build neural highways through repetition that provide efficient access to Y.O.D.A.'s wisdom and insights (e.g. "The way I speak to my children will one day be the way they speak to themselves, their inner coach").

- Record the public messages (tone and content) you send to your children, both good and bad, on a given day. What are the key messages you want to upload into your child's inner core that will be with them throughout their lives, until their death?

- What coaching advice do you have for yourself in summoning wisdom and perspective (Y.O.D.A.) when the next major crisis erupts with you, your child, or your teen?

- Write three to five words that most accurately depict who you most want to be with family members, and place those words in a prominent place in your home.

- Every investment of energy spawns life. Determine what you most want to grow in yourself and in the members of your family. Develop a specific energy investment plan and make a conscious effort to invest every day.

- Describe your three most effective stress management decision-making tools. Consider how stress exposure may actually be a gift to you in acquiring wisdom over time.

- Reflect on your last flow experience, and consider how your understanding of flow could contribute to better decision-making.

- Give a concrete example from your own life that supports the following statement:

     "More important than what happens to me in life is the story I create about what happens."

In what way does your story impact your ability to make wise decisions?

- Purchase a journal and script how you want your inner voice to coach you in situations that have historically caused your private voice to turn negative and even perhaps abusive. Reflect on how you would advise a child, family member, or close friend about whom you care deeply in the very same situation. Would you ever speak to them the way you speak to yourself? Write for 10 minutes a day for three weeks, and then assess any positive changes that have occurred in how you coach yourself and how those changes have impacted your ability to make better decisions.

- Consider what you would most want inscribed on your tombstone to reflect who you really were when you were alive. The words you choose represent what getting home in your life really means. What decisions must you make to ensure getting home becomes a reality?

- Ensure every major decision you make is fully aligned with your ultimate mission in life:

     Getting home!

SOURCES

INTRODUCTION

Augenblick, N., and S. Nicholson. "Ballot Position, Choice Fatigue, and Voter Behavior." July 2011. Retrieved from http://faculty.haas.berkeley.edu/ned/Choice_Fatigue.pdf

Baumeister, R. F., E. Bratslavsky, M. Muraven, and D. M. Tice. "Ego Depletion: Is the Active Self a Limited Resource?" *Journal of Personality and Social Psychology* 74, no. 5 (1998): 1252–1265.

Bond, S. T., K. A. Carlson, and R. L. Keeney. "Improving the Generation of Decision Objectives." *Decision Analysis* 7 (2010): 238–255.

Brehm, J. W. "A Brief History of Dissonance Theory." *Social and Personality Psychology Compass* 1 (2007): 381–391.

De Smet, A., G. Jost, and L. Weiss. "Three Keys to Faster, Better Decisions." *McKinsey Quarterly*, May 1, 2019.

Edwards, W. "The Theory of Decision Making." *Psychological Bulletin* 51 (1954): 380–417.

Festinger, L. "Cognitive Dissonance." *Scientific American* 207 (1962): 93–102.

Gailliot, M. T., and R. F. Baumeister. "The Physiology of Willpower: Linking Blood Glucose to Self-Control. "*Personality and Social Psychology Bulletin* 11, no. 4 (2007): 303–327.

Gilovich, T., D. Griffin, and D. Kahneman. *Heuristics and Biases: The Psychology of Intuitive Judgment*. Cambridge: Cambridge University Press, 2002.

Hammond, J. S., R. L. Keeney, and H. Raiffa. *Smart Choices, A Practical Guide to Making Better Decisions*. Boston: Harvard Business School Press, 1999.

Heath, C., and D. Heath. *Decisive: How to Make Better Choices in Life and Work*. New York: Crown Business, 2013

Kahneman, D., P. Slovic, and A. Tversky. *Judgment under Uncertainty: Heuristics and Biases*. Cambridge: Cambridge University Press, 1982.

Keeney, R. L. *Give Yourself a Nudge: Helping Smart People Make Smarter Personal and Business Decisions*. Cambridge, UK: Cambridge University Press, 2020.

Keeney, R. L. "Personal Decisions Are the Leading Cause of Death." *Operations Research* 56 (2008): 1335–1347.

Keeney, R. L., and A. B. Palley. "Decision Strategies to Reduce Teenage and Young Adult Deaths in The United States." *Risk Analysis* 33 (2013): 1661–1676.

Laran, J., and C. Janiszewski. "Work or Fun? How Task Construal and Completion Influence Regulatory Behavior." *Journal of Consumer Research* 37 (2011): 967–983.

Latham, A. "12 Reasons Why How You Make Decisions Is More Important Than What You Decide." *Forbes*, November 15, 2015.

March, J. G. *A Primer on Decision Making: How Decisions Happen.* New York: Free Press, 1994

Nickerson, R. S. "Confirmation Bias: A Ubiquitous Phenomenon in Many Guises." *Review of General Psychology* 2 (1988): 175–220. doi: 10.1037 /1089-2680.2.2.175

Oswald, M. E., and S. Grosjean. "Confirmation Bias." In R. F. Pohl (Ed.), *Cognitive Illusions: A Handbook on Fallacies and Biases in Thinking, Judgement and Memory*, pp. 79–96. Hove, UK: Psychology Press, 2004.

Rose, T. *Collective Illusions: Conformity, Complicity, and the Science of Why We Make Bad Decisions.* New York: Hachette Books, 2022.

Samuelson, W., and R. Zeckhauser. "Status Quo Bias in Decision Making." *Journal of Risk and Uncertainty* 1 (1988): 7–59.

Schmeichel, B. J., K. D. Vohs, and R. F. Baumeister. "Intellectual Performance and Ego Depletion: Role of the Self in Logical Reasoning and Other Information Processing." *Journal of Personality and Social Psychology* 85, no. 1 (2003): 33–46.

Simon, H. "A Behavioral Model of Rational Choice." *Quarterly Journal of Economics* 69 (1955): 99–118.

Soll, J. B., K. L. Milkman, and J. W. Payne. "Outsmart Your Own Biases." *Harvard Business Review* 93 (2015): 64–71.

Tversky, A., and D. Kahneman. "Judgment Under Uncertainty: Heuristics and Biases." *Science* 185 (1974): 1124–1131.

Vohs, K. D., R. F. Baumeister, B. J. Schmeichel, J. M. Twenge, N. M. Nelson, and D. M. Tice. "Making Choices Impairs Subsequent Self-Control: A Limited-Resource Account of Decision Making, Self-Regulation, and Active Initiative." *Journal of Personality and Social Psychology* 94, no. 5 (2008): 883–898.

Westen, D., P. S. Blagov, K. Harenski, C. Kilts, and S. Hamann. "Neural Bases of Motivated Reasoning: An fMRI Study of Emotional Constraints on Partisan Political Judgment in the 2004 U.S. Presidential Election." *Journal of Cognitive Neuroscience* 18 (2006): 1947–1958.

CHAPTER 1

Borwick, C., R. Lal, L. W. Lim, C. J. Stagg, and L. Aquili. "Dopamine Depletion Effects on Cognitive Flexibility as Modulated by tDCS of the dlPFC." *Brain Stimulation* 13, no. 1 (2020): 105–108.

Boyce, W. T. *The Orchid and the Dandelion: Why Some Children Struggle and How All Can Thrive.* New York: Knopf, 2019.

Burnett, C., E. Purkey, C. M. Davison, A. Watson, J. Kehoe, S. Traviss, D. Nolan, and I. Bayoumi. "Spirituality, Community Belonging, and Mental Health Outcomes of Indigenous Peoples During the Covid-19 Pandemic." *International Journal of Environmental Research and Public Health* 19, no. 4 (2022): 2472.

Chekroud, S. R., R. Gueorguieva, A. B. Zheutlin, M. Paulus, H. M. Krumholz, J. H. Krystal, and A. M. Chekroud. "Association between Physical Exercise and Mental Health in 1.2 Million Individuals in the USA between 2011 and 2015: A Cross-Sectional Study." *Lancet Psychiatry* 5, no. 9 (2018): 739–746.

Damasio, A. R. *The Strange Order of Things: Life, Feeling, and the Making of the Cultures.* New York: Pantheon Books, 2018.

Dossett, M. L., G. L. Fricchione, and H. Benson. "A New Era for Mind-Body Medicine." *New England Journal of Medicine* 382, no. 15 (2020): 1390–1391.

Fogg, B. J. *Tiny Habits: The Small Changes That Change Everything.* Boston: Houghton Mifflin Harcourt, 2019.

Gershon, M. D. *The Second Brain: A Groundbreaking New Understanding of Nervous Disorders of the Stomach and Intestine.* New York: Harper Collins, 1998.

Heinrichs, M., and G. Domes. "Neuropeptides and Social Behavior: Effects of Oxytocin and Vasopressin in Humans." *Progress in Brain Research* 170 (2008): 337–350.

Inagaki, T. K., L. A. Ray, M. R. Irwin, B. M. Way, and N. I. Eisenberger. "Opioids and Social Bonding: Naltrexone Reduces Feelings of Social Connection." *Social Cognitive and Affective Neuroscience* 11, no. 5 (2016): 728–735.

Kanherkar, R. R., N. Bhatia-Dey, and A. B. Csoka. "Epigenetics across the Human Lifespan." *Frontiers in Cell and Developmental Biology* 2 (2014): 49.

Kashdan, T. B., and J. Rottenberg. "Psychological Flexibility as a Fundamental Aspect of Health." *Clinical Psychology Review* 30, no. 7 (2010): 865–878.

Koenig, H. G. "Religion, Spirituality, and Health: The Research and Clinical Implications." *ISRN Psychiatry* (2012). doi: 10.5402/2012/278730

Mandolesi, L., A. Polverino, S. Montuori, F. Foti, G. Ferraioli, P. Sorrentino, and G. Sorrentino. "Effects of Physical Exercise on Cognitive Functioning and Wellbeing: Biological and Psychological Benefits." *Frontiers in Psychology* 9 (2018): 509.

McEwen, B. S. "Central Effects of Stress Hormones in Health and Disease: Understanding the Protective and Damaging Effects of Stress and Stress Mediators." *European Journal of Pharmacology* 583, no. 2–3 (2008): 174–185.

Meyer-Lindenberg, A., G. Domes, P. Kirsch, and M. Heinrichs. "Oxytocin and Vasopressin in the Human Brain: Social Neuropeptides for Translational Medicine." *Nature Reviews Neurosciences* 12, no. 9 (2011): 524–538.

Neumann, I. D. "Oxytocin: The Neuropeptide of Love Reveals Some of Its Secrets." *Cell Metabolism* 5, no. 4 (2007): 231–233.

Pert, C. B. *Molecules of Emotion: The Science Behind Mind-Body Medicine.* New York: Touchstone, 1997.

Plomin, R. *Behavioral Genetics*, 4th ed. New York: Worth, 2001.

Ratey, J. J., and E. Hagerman. *Spark: The Revolutionary New Science of Exercise and the Brain*. New York: Little, Brown, 2008.

Rea, I. M., D. S. Gibson, V. McGilligan, S. E. McNerlan, H. D. Alexander, and O. A. Ross. "Age and Age-Related Diseases: Role of Inflammation Triggers and Cytokines." *Frontiers in Immunology* 9 (2018): 586.

Shonkoff, J. P., D. A. Phillips, and National Research Council (U.S.). Committee on Integrating the Science of Early Childhood Development. *From Neurons to Neighborhoods: The Science of Early Child Development*. Washington, D.C.: National Academy Press, 2000.

Smith, P. A. "The Tantalizing Links between Gut Microbes and the Brain." *Nature* 526, no. 7573 (2015): 312–314.

Sullivan, E. V., R. A. Harris, and A. Pfefferbaum. "Alcohol's Effects on Brain and Behavior." *Alcohol Research & Health* 33, no. 1–2 (2010): 127–143.

Tanaka, T., M. Narazaki, and T. Kishimoto. "Il-6 in Inflammation, Immunity, and Disease." *Cold Spring Harbor Perspectives in Biology* 6, no. 10 (2014): a016295.

Tronick, E., and R. G. Hunter. "Waddington, Dynamic Systems, and Epigenetics." *Frontiers in Behavioral Neuroscience* 10 (2016): 107.

Waldinger, R. J., and M. S. Schulz. "What's Love Got to Do with It? Social Functioning, Perceived Health, and Daily Happiness in Married Octogenarians." *Psychology and Aging* 25 no. 2 (2010): 422–431.

Wells, G. 2017. *The Ripple Effect: Sleep Better, Eat Better, Move Better, Think Better*. Toronto, Ontario: Collins.

Young, S. N. "How to Increase Serotonin in the Human Brain without Drugs." *Journal of Psychiatry & Neuroscience* 32, no. 6 (2007): 394–399.

Yu, R. "Stress Potentiates Decision Biases: A Stress Induced Deliberation-to-Intuition (Sidi) Model." *Neurobiology of Stress* 3 (2016): 83–95.

CHAPTER 2

Banas, J., and S. Rains. "A Meta-Analysis of Research on Inoculation Theory." *Communication Monographs* 77, no. 3 (2010): 281–311. https://doi.org/10.1080/03637751003758193

Beutler, L. E., C. Moleiro, and H. Talebi. "Resistance in Psychotherapy: What Conclusions Are Supported by Research." *Journal of Clinical Psychology* 58 (2002): 207–217.

Bonetto, E., J. Trian, F. Varet, G. L. Monaco, and F. Girandola. "Priming Resistance to Persuasion Decreases Adherence to Conspiracy Theories." *Social Influence* 13, no. 3 (2018): 125–136. https://doi.org/10.1080

Cautilli, J. D., T. C. Riley-Tillman, S. Axelrod, and P. N. Hineline. "Current Behavioral Models of Client and Consultee Resistance: A Critical Review." *International Journal of Behavioral Consultation and Therapy* 1 (2005): 147–154.

Cautilli, J. D., and L. Santilli-Connor. "Assisting the Client/Consultee to Do What Is Needed." A Functional Analysis of Resistance and Other Forms of Avoidance." *Behavior Analyst Today* 1 (2000): 37–42.

Conway, K. "Encoding/Decoding as Translation." *International Journal of Communication* 11 (2017): 18.

Craig, A. D. "How Do You Feel—Now? The Anterior Insula and Human Awareness." *Nature Reviews Neuroscience*, 10 (2009): 59–70.

Ecker, U. K. H., S. Lewandowsky, B. Swire, and D. Chang. "Misinformation in Memory: Effects of the Encoding Strength and Strength of Retraction." Manuscript submitted for publication, 2010.

Fein, S., A. L. McCloskey, and T. M. Tomlinson. "Can the Jury Disregard that Information? The Use of Suspicion to Reduce the Prejudicial Effects of Pretrial Publicity and Inadmissible Testimony." *Personality & Social Psychology Bulletin* 23 (1997): 1215–1226.

Frederick, S. "Cognitive Reflection and Decision Making." *Journal of Economic Perspectives* 19, no. 4 (2005): 25–42.

Gilbert, D. T., D. S. Krull, and P. S. Malone. "Unbelieving the Unbelievable: Some Problems in the Rejection of False Information." *Journal of Personality & Social Psychology* 59 (1990): 601–613.

Gilbert, D. T., R. W. Tafarodi, and P. S. Malone. "You Can't Not Believe Everything You Read." *Journal of Personality & Social Psychology* 65 (1993): 221–233.

Greene, E., M. S. Flynn, and E. F. Loftus. "Inducing Resistance to Misleading Information." *Journal of Verbal Learning & Verbal Behavior* 21 (1982): 207–219.

Luntz, F. *Words That Work: It's Not What You Say, It's What People Hear.* New York: Hyperion, 2007.

McCabe, D. P., and A. D. Smith. "The Effect of Warnings on False Memories in Young and Older Adults." *Memory & Cognition* 30 (2002): 1065–1077.

McDermott, K. B. "The Persistence of False Memories in List Recall." *Journal of Memory & Language* 35 (1996): 212–230.

Messer, S. B. "A Psychodynamic Perspective on Resistance in Psychotherapy: Vive la Resistance." *Journal of Clinical Psychology* 58 (2002): 157–163.

Patterson, G. R., and P. Chamberlain. "A Functional Analysis of Resistance During Parent Training." *Clinical Psychology: Science and Practice* 1 (1994): 53–70.

Rohini, A. "Examination of Psychological Processes Underlying Resistance to Persuasion." *Journal of Consumer Research* 27, no. 2 (2000): 217–232.

Saywitz, K. J., and S. Moan-Hardie. "Reducing the Potential for Distortion of Childhood Memories." *Consciousness & Cognition* 3 (1994): 408–425.

Seamon, J. G., C. R. Luo, J. J. Kopecky, C. A. Price, L. Rothschild, N. S. Fung, and M. A. Schwartz. "Are False Memories More Difficult to Forget than Accurate Memories? The Effect of Retention Interval on Recall and Recognition." *Memory & Cognition* 30 (2002): 1054–1064.

Uddin, L. Q., J. S. Nomi, B. Hebert-Seropian, J. Ghazi, and O. Boucher. "Structure and Function of the Human Insula." *Journal of Clinical Neurophysiology* 34, no. 4 (2017): 300–306.

Van Denburg, T. F., and D. J. Kiesler. "An Interpersonal Communication Perspective on Resistance in Psychotherapy." *Journal of Clinical Psychology* 58 (2002): 195–205.

Warren, A., K. Hulse-Trotter, and E. C. Tubbs. "Inducing Resistance to Suggestibility in Children." *Law & Human Behavior* 15 (1991): 273–285.

Watson, J. M., K. B. McDermott, and D. A. Balota. (2004). "Attempting to Avoid False Memories in the Deese/Roediger–McDermott Paradigm: Assessing the Combined Influence of Practice and Warnings in Young and Old Adults." *Memory & Cognition* 32 (2004): 135–141.

Westerberg, C. E., and C. J. Marsolek. "Do Instructional Warnings Reduce False Recognition?" *Applied Cognitive Psychology* 20 (2006): 97–114.

CHAPTER 3

Carruthers, P. "The Cognitive Functions of Language." *Behavioral and Brain Sciences* 25 (2002): 657–726.

Kross, E. *Chatter, The Voice in Our Head, Why It Matters, and How to Harness It.* New York: Random House, 2021.

Emerson, M. J., and A. Miyake. "The Role of Inner Speech in Task Switching: A Dual-Task Investigation." *Journal of Memory and Language* 48 (2003): 148–168.

Fernyhough, C. *The Voices Within: The History and Science of How We Talk to Ourselves*. New York: Basic Books, 2016.

Finn, J. A. "Competitive Excellence: It's a Matter of Mind and Body." *Physician and Sportsmedicine* 13 (1985): 61–75.

Gathercole, S. E., and A. D. Baddeley. *Working Memory and Language*. Hove, UK: Erlbaum, 1993.

Gentner, D., and S. Goldin-Meadow (Eds.). *Language in Mind: Advances in the Study of Language and Thought*. Cambridge, MA: MIT Press, 2003.

Gould, D., R. C. Eklund, and S. A. Jackson. "1988 U.S. Olympic Wrestling Excellence: II. Thoughts and Affect Occurring During Competition." *Sport Psychologist* 6 (1992): 383–402.

Gruber, O., and T. Goschke. "Executive Control Emerging from Dynamic Interactions between Brain Systems Mediating Language, Working Memory and Attentional Processes." *Acta Psychologica* 115 (2004): 105–121.

Hardy, J. "Speaking Clearly: A Critical Review of the Self-Talk Literature." *Psychology of Sport & Exercise* 7 (2006): 81–97.

Hardy, J., K. Gammage, and C. R. Hall. "A Descriptive Study of an Athlete's Self-Talk." *Sport Psychologist* 15 (2011): 306–318.

Hardy, J., C. R. Hall, and L. Hardy. "Quantifying Self-Talk." *Journal of Sports Sciences* 23 (2005): 905–917.

Harvey, D. T., J. L. Van Raalte, and B. W. Brewer. "Relationship between Self-Talk and Golf Performance." *International Sports Journal* 6 (2002): 84–91.

Hatzigeorgiadis, A. "Instructional and Motivational Self-Talk: An Investigation on Perceived Self-Talk Functions." *Hellenic Journal of Psychology* 3 (2006): 164–175.

Hatzigeorgiadis, A., Y. Theodorkis, and N. Zourbanos. "Self-Talk in the Swimming Pool: The Effects of Self-Talk on Thought Content and Performance on Water-Polo Tasks." *Journal of Applied Sport Psychology* 16 (2004): 138–150.

Hatzigeorgiadis, A., N. Zourbanos, and Y. Theodorakis. "An Examination on the Moderating Effects of Self-Talk Content on Self-Talk Functions." *Journal of Applied Sport Psychology* 19 (2007): 241–250.

Johnson, J. J. M., D. W. Hrycaiko, G. V. Johnson, and J. M. Hallas. "Self-Talk and Female Youth Soccer Performance." *Sport Psychologist* 18 (2004): 44–59.

Landin, D., and E. P. Hebert. "The Influence of Self-Talk on the Performance of Skilled Female Tennis Players." *Journal of Applied Sport Psychology* 11 (1999): 263–282.

Lazarus, R. S. "Thoughts on the Relation Between Emotion and Cognition." *American Psychologist* 37 (1982): 1019–1024.

Luria, A. R. *The Role of Speech in the Regulation of Normal and Abnormal Behavior*. New York: Liveright, 1961.

Perkos, S., Y. Theodorakis, and S. Chroni. "Enhancing Performance and Skill Acquisition in Novice Basketball Players with Instructional Self-Talk." *Sport Psychologist* 16 (2002): 368–383.

Peters, H. J., and J. M. Williams. *What Type of Self-Talk Do Athletes Believe Help and Hurt Their Performance?* Poster Presented at the Meeting of the Association for the Advancement of Applied Sport Psychology, Philadelphia, 2003.

Ramirez, J. D. "The Functional Differentiation of Social and Private Speech: A Dialogic Approach." In R. M. Diaz and L. E. Berk (Eds.), *Private Speech: From Social Interaction to Self-Regulation.* Hillsdale, NJ: Erlbaum, 1992.

Rushall, B. S., M. Hall, L. Roux, J. Sasseville, and A. C. Rushall. "Effects of Three Types of Thought Content Instructions on Skiing Performance." *Sport Psychologist* 2 (1988): 283–297.

Theodorakis, Y., S. Chroni, K. Laparidis, V. Bebestos, and I. Douma. "Self-Talk in a Basketball-Shooting Task." *Perceptual and Motor Skills* 92 (2001): 309–315.

Theodorakis, Y., R. Weinberg, P. Natsis, I. Douma, and P. Kazakas. "The Effects of Motivational and Instructional Self-Talk on Improving Motor Performance." *Sport Psychologist* 14 (2000): 253–271.

Van Noorde, N. L. *Development and Evaluation of a Self-Talk Assessment Instrument for Tennis Players.* Unpublished doctoral dissertation, Michigan State University, East Lansing, MI, 1984.

Van Raalte, J. L., B. W. Brewer, B. P. Lewis, D. E. Linder, G. Wildman, and J. Kozimor. "Cork! The Effects of Positive and Negative Self-Talk on Dart Performance." *Journal of Sport Behavior* 3 (1995): 50–57.

Van Raalte, J. L., B. W. Brewer, P. M. Rivera, and A. J. Petitpas. "The Relationship between Observable Self-Talk and Competitive Junior Players' Match Performances." *Journal of Sport and Exercise Psychology* 16 (1994): 400–415.

Van Raalte, J. L., A. E. Cornelius, B. W. Brewer, and S. J. Hatton. "The Antecedents and Consequences of Self-Talk in Competitive Tennis." *Journal of Sport and Exercise Psychology* 22 (2000): 345–356.

Vygotsky, L. *Thought and Language* (A. Kozulin, Trans.). Cambridge, MA: MIT Press, 1986 (Original work published in 1934).

Vygotsky, L. *Thinking and Speech: The Collected Works of Lev Vygotsky,* vol. 1. New York: Plenum Press, 1987.

Weinberg, R. S., J. Smith, A. Jackson, and D. Gould. "Effect of Association, Dissociation, and Positive Self-Talk on Endurance Performance." *Canadian Journal of Applied Sport Sciences* 9 (1984): 25–32.

Chapter 4

Ackerman, C. E. "What is Self-Image and How Do We Improve It? Definition + Quotes," *Positive Psychology* 2002, https://positivepsychology.com/self-image/

Blakemore, S.-J., and Frith, C. "Self-Awareness and Action." *Current Opinion in Neurobiology* 13, no. 2 (2003): 219–224.

Carver, C. S. "Self-Awareness." In M. R. Leary and J. P. Tangney (Eds.), *Handbook of Self and Identity*, pp. 50–68. New York: Guilford Press, 2012.

Cherry, K. "What is Self-Awareness?" *Verywell Mind*, 2020, https://www.verywellmind.com/what-is-self-awareness-2795023

Gur, R. C. and H. A. Sackeim. "Self-Deception: A Concept in Search of a Phenomenon." *Journal of Personality and Social Psychology* 37 (1979): 147–169.

Morin, A. "Self-Awareness Part 1: Definition, Measures, Effects, Functions, and Antecedents." *Social and Personality Psychology Compass* 5, no. 10 (2011): 807–823.

Morin, A., and J. Everett. "Inner Speech as a Mediator of Self-Awareness, Self-Consciousness, and Self-Knowledge: An Hypothesis." *New Ideas in Psychology* 8 (1990): 337–356.

Morin, A., and J. Everett. "Self-Awareness and 'Introspective' Private Speech in 6-Year-Old Children." *Psychological Reports* 68 (1990): 1299–1306.

Mossman, J. "Strong Opinions." BBC interview. Cited in *Vladimir Nabokov*. New York: Vintage, 1990.

Rochat, P. "Five Levels of Self-Awareness as They Unfold Early in Life." *Consciousness and Cognition* 12, no. 4 (2003): 717–731.

Roessler, J. "Thinking, Inner Speech, and Self-Awareness." *Review of Philosophy and Psychology* 7 (2015): 541–557.

Chapter 5

Adams, J. S., A. Tashchian, and T. H. Shore. "Codes of Ethics as Signals for Ethical Behavior." *Journal of Business Ethics* 29 (2001): 199–211.

Ariely, D. *The Honest Truth About Dishonesty: How We Lie to Everyone—Especially Ourselves*. New York: HarperCollins, 2012.

Baron-Cohen, S. *The Science of Evil*. New York: Basic Books, 2011.

Baumgartner, T., M. Heinrichs, A. Vonlanthen, U. Fishbacher, and E. Febre. "Kindness and Other Prosocial Acts Such as Empathy and Compassion are Associated with Elevated Levels of the Hormone Oxytocin." *Neuron* 58, no. 4 (2008): 639–650.

Bayer, M. *Best Self*. New York: HarperCollins, 2019.

Bazerman, M. H., and A. E. Tenbrunsel. *Blind Spots: Why We Fail to Do What's Right and What to Do About It*. Princeton, NJ: Princeton University Press, 2011.

Bazerman, M. H., A. E. Tenbrunsel, and K. Wade-Benzoni. "Negotiating with Yourself and Losing: Making Decisions with Competing Internal Preferences." *Academy of Management Review* 23 (1998): 225–241.

Bersoff, D. "Why Good People Sometimes Do Bad Things: Motivated Reasoning and Unethical Behavior." *Personality and Social Psychology Bulletin* 25 (1999): 28–39.

Brooks, A. C. *From Strength to Strength: Finding Success, Happiness, and Deep Purpose in the Second Half of Life*. New York: Portfolio/Penguin, 2022.

Caslen, R., and M. Matthews. *The Character Edge: Leading and Winning with Integrity*. New York: St. Martin's Press, 2020.

Covey, S. R., and R. M. Rebecca. *The Speed of Trust: The One Thing that Changes Everything*. New York: Simon and Schuster, 2006.

Das, G. *The Difficulty of Being Good*. New York: Oxford University Press, 2009.

DeCelles, K. A., D. S. DeRue, J. D. Margolis, and T. L. Ceranic. "Does Power Corrupt or Enable? When and Why Power Facilitates Self-Interested Behavior." *Journal of Applied Psychology* 7 (2012): 681–689.

Decety, J., K. J. Michalska, and K. D. Kinzler. "The Developmental Neuroscience of Moral Sensitivity." *Emotion Review* 3 (2011): 305–307.

Deci, E. L. *The Psychology of Self-Determination*. Lexington, MA: Lexington Books, D.C. Heath, 1980.

de Waal, E. *Good Natured: The Origins of Right and Wrong in Humans and Other Animals*. Cambridge, MA: Harvard University Press, 1996.

Flack, J. C., and F. de Waal. "Being Nice Is Not a Building-Block of Morality." *Journal of Consciousness Studies* 7 (2000): 67–78.

Forte, A. "Antecedents of Managers' Moral Reasoning." *Journal of Business Ethics* 51 (2004): 315–347.

Gellennan, S. W. "Why 'Good' Managers Make Bad Ethical Choices." *Harvard Business Review* (July–August 1986): 85–90.

Gino, F. "Understanding Ordinary Unethical Behavior Why People Who Value Morality Act Immorally." *Behavioral Sciences* 3 (2015): 107–111.

Gino, F., and A. D. Galinsky. "Vicarious Dishonesty: When Psychology Closeness Creates Distance from One's Moral Compass." *Organizational Behavior and Human Decision Processes* 119 (2012): 15–26.

Graham, J., B. A. Nosek, J. Haidt, R. Iyer, S., Koleva, and P. H. Ditto. "Mapping the Moral Domain." *Journal of Personality and Social Psychology* 101 (2011): 366–385.

Grant, A. *Give and Take*. New York: Penguin Books, 2014.

Haidt, J. *The Righteous Mind: Why Good People Are Divided by Politics and Religion*. New York: Pantheon, 2012.

Hauser, M. *Moral Minds: How Nature Designed Our Universal Sense of Right and Wrong*. New York: Ecco, 2006.

Hogeveen, J., M. Inzlicht, and S. S. Obhi. "Power Changes How the Brain Responds to Others." *Journal of Experimental Psychology: General* 143 (2014): 755–762.

Huebner, B., S. Dwyer, and M. Hauser. "The Role of Emotion in Moral Psychology." *Trends in Cognitive Sciences* 13 (2009): 1–6.

Kabat-Zinn, J. *Wherever You Go, There You Are: Mindfulness Meditation in Everyday Life*. New York: Hyperion, 1994.

Keltner, D., and J. Haidt. "Approaching Awe, A Moral, Spiritual, and Aesthetic Emotion." *Cognition and Emotion* 17 (2003): 297–314.

Kern, M., and D. Chugh. "Bounded Ethically: The Perils of Loss Framing." *Psychological Science* 20 (2009): 378–384.

Lee, J. J., F. Gino, E. S. Jim, L. K. Rice, and R. A. Josephs. "Hormones and Ethics: Understanding the Biological Basis of Unethical Conduct." *Journal of Experimental Psychology: General* 144 (2015): 891–897.

Loehr, J. *The Only Way to Win: How Building Character Drives Higher Achievement and Greater Fulfillment in Business and Life*. New York: Hyperion, 2012.

Loehr, J., and C. Kenny. *Leading with Character, 10 Minutes a Day to a Brilliant Legacy*. Hoboken, NJ: Wiley, 2020.

Newberg, A., and M. Waldman. *Why Believe What We Believe: Uncovering Our Biological Need for Meaning, Spirituality, and Truth*. New York: Free Press, 2006.

Peterson, C., and M. Seligman. *Character Strengths and Virtues*. New York: Oxford University Press, 2004.

Rand, A. *Philosophy: Who Needs It*. New York: Bobbs-Merrill, 1982, p.6.

Ruedy, E., C. Moore, F. Gino, and M. E. Schweitzer. "The Cheater's High: The Unexpected Affective Benefits of Unethical Behavior." *Journal of Personality and Social Psychology* 105 (2013): 531–548.

Seligman, M. *Flourish: A Visionary New Understanding of Happiness and Well-Being*. New York: Nicholas Brealey, 2011.

Shalvi, S., F. Gino, R. Barkan, and S. Ayal. "Self-Serving Justifications: Doing Wrong and Feeling Moral." *Current Directions in Psychological Science* 24 (2015): 125–130.

Smith, A. *The Theory of Moral Sentiments*. Exercere Cerebrum Publications, 2014.

Strecher, V. *Life on Purpose: How Living for What Matters Most Changes Everything*. New York: HarperCollins, 2016.

Tenbrunsel, A. E., and K. Smith-Crowe. "Ethical Decision Making: Where We've Been and Where We're Going." *Academy of Management Annals* 2 (2008): 545–607.

Tenbrunsel, A. E., and D. M. Messick. "Ethical Fading: The Role of Self-Deception in Unethical Behavior." *Social Justice Research* 17 (2004): 223–236.

Waller, J. *Becoming Evil*. Oxford, UK: Oxford University Press, 2007.

Warren, D., J. Gaspar, and W. Laufer. "Is Formal Ethics Training Merely Cosmetic? A Study of Ethics Training and Ethical Organizational Culture." *Business Ethics Quarterly* 24 (2014): 85–117.

CHAPTER 6

Ackerman, R., and A. T. Valerie. "Meta-Reasoning: Monitoring and Control of Thinking and Reasoning." *Trends in Cognitive Sciences* 21, no. 8 (2017): 607–617.

Banas, J., and S. Rains. "A Meta-Analysis of Research on Inoculation Theory." *Communication Monographs* 77, no. 3 (2010): 281–311. https://doi.org/10.1080/03637751003758193

Baumeister, R. F., E. Bratslavsky, C. Finkenauer, and K. D. Vohs. "Bad Is Stronger than Good." *Review of General Psychology* 5, no. 4 (2001): 323–370.

Beutler, L. E., C. Moleiro, and H. Talebi. "Resistance in Psychotherapy: What Conclusions Are Supported by Research." *Journal of Clinical Psychology* 58 (2002): 207–217.

Bonetto, E., J. Trian, F. Varet, G. L. Monaco, and F. Girandola. "Priming Resistance to Persuasion Decreases Adherence to Conspiracy Theories." *Social Influence* 13, no. 3 (2018): 125–136. doi.org/10.1080/15534510.2018.1471415

Cautilli, J. D., and L. Santilli-Connor. "Assisting the Client/Consultee to Do What Is Needed. A Functional Analysis of Resistance and Other Forms of Avoidance." *Behavior Analyst Today* 1 (2000): 37–42.

Dunning, D. *Self-Insight: Roadblocks and Detours on the Path to Knowing Thyself*. New York: Psychology Press, 2012.

Dweck, C. 2016. *Mindset: The New Psychology of Success*. New York: Ballantine Books.

Greene, E., M. S. Flynn, and E. F. Loftus. "Inducing Resistance to Misleading Information." *Journal of Verbal Learning & Verbal Behavior* 21 (1982): 207–219.

Johnson, M. K., and C. L. Raye. "Reality Monitoring." *Psychological Review* 88, no. 1 (1981): 67.

Lewandowsky, S., W. G. K. Stritzke, K. Oberauer, and M. Morales. "Memory for Fact, Fiction, and Misinformation: The Iraq War 2003." *Psychological Science* 16 (2005): 190–195.

Patterson, G. R., and P. Chamberlain. "A Functional Analysis of Resistance during Parent Training." *Clinical Psychology: Science and Practice* 1 (1994): 53–70.

Rohini, A. "Examination of Psychological Processes Underlying Resistance to Persuasion." *Journal of Consumer Research* 27, no. 2 (2000): 217–232.

Scott, R. M., and R. Baillargeon. "Early False-Belief Understanding." *Trends in Cognitive Sciences* 21, no. 4 (2017): 237–249.

Seligman, M. E. *Learned Optimism: How to Change Your Mind and Your Life.* New York: Vintage, 2006.

Tavris, C., and E. Aronso. *Mistakes Were Made (But Not by Me): Why We Justify Foolish Beliefs, Bad Decisions, and Hurtful Acts,* New York: Houghton Mifflin Harcourt, 2007.

Warren, A., K. Hulse-Trotter, and E. C. Tubbs. "Inducing Resistance to Suggestibility in Children." *Law & Human Behavior* 15 (1991): 273–285.

Wilson, T. D., and N. Brekke. "Mental Contamination and Mental Correction: Unwanted Influences on Judgments and Evaluations." *Psychological Bulletin* 116 (1994): 117–142.

CHAPTER 7

Alexander, R., O. R. Aragon, J. Bookwala, N. Cherbuin, J. M. Gatt, I. J. Kahrilas, N. Kastner, A. Lawrence, L. Lowe, R. G. Morrison, S. C. Mueller, R. Nusslock, C. Papadelis, K. L. Polnaszek, S. Helene Richter, R. L. Silton, and C. Styliadis. "The Neuroscience of Positive Emotions and Affect: Implications for Cultivating Happiness and Wellbeing." *Neuroscience & Biobehavioral Reviews* 121 (2021): 220–249.

Bell, C., C. Bourke, H. Colhoun, F. Carter, C. Frampton, and R. Porter. "The Misclassification of Facial Expressions in Generalised Social Phobia." *Journal of Anxiety Disorders* 25, no. 2 (2011): 278–283.

Borysenko, J. *Minding the Body, Mending the Mind.* New York MJF Books, 2014.

Brackett, M. *Permission to Feel.* New York: Celadon Books, 2019.

Cantor, P., D. Osher, J. Berg, L. Steyer, and T. Rose. "Malleability, Plasticity, and Individuality: How Children Learn and Develop in Context." *Applied Developmental Science* 23, no. 4, (2019): 307–337.

Davidson, R. J., and S. Begley. *The Emotional Life of Your Brain: How Its Unique Patterns Affect the Way You Think, Feel, and Live—and How You Can Change Them*. New York: Hudson Street Press, 2012.

Dishon, N., J. A. Oldmeadow, C. Critchley, and J. Kaufman. "The Effect of Trait Self-Awareness, Self-Reflection, and Perceptions of Choice Meaningfulness on Indicators of Social Identity within a Decision-Making Context." *Frontiers in Psychology* 8 (2017): 2034.

Immordino-Yang, M. H., J. A. Christodoulou, and V. Singh. "Rest Is Not Idleness: Implications of the Brain's Default Mode for Human Development and Education." *Perspectives on Psychological Science* 7, no. 4 (2012): 352–364.

Immordino-Yang, M. H., L. Darling-Hammond, and C. Krone. "The Brain Basis for Integrated Social, Emotional, and Academic Development." The Aspen Institute, National Commission on Social, Emotional and Academic Development, 2018.

Jaaskelainen, I. P., V. Klucharev, K. Panidi, and A. N. Shestakova. "Neural Processing of Narratives: From Individual Processing to Viral Propagation." *Frontiers in Human Neuroscience* 14 (2020): 253.

Jeong, J., E. E. Franchett, C. V. Ramos de Oliveira, K. Rehmani, and A. K. Yousafzai. "Parenting Interventions to Promote Early Child Development in the First Three Years of Life: A Global Systematic Review and Meta-Analysis." *PLoS Med* 18, no. 5, (2021): e1003602.

Johnson, S. B., A. W. Riley, D. A. Granger, and J. Riis. "The Science of Early Life Toxic Stress for Pediatric Practice and Advocacy." *Pediatrics* 131, no. 2 (2013): 319–327.

Kaller, M. S., A. Lazari, C. Blanco-Duque, C. Sampaio-Baptista, and H. Johansen-Berg. "Myelin Plasticity and Behavior—Connecting the Dots." *Current Opinion in Neurobiology* 47 (2017): 86–92.

Kaplan, J. T., S. I. Gimbel, M. Dehghani, M. H. Immordino-Yang, K. Sagae, J. D. Wong, C. M. Tipper, H. Damasio, A. S. Gordon, and A. Damasio. "Processing Narratives Concerning Protected Values: A Cross-Cultural Investigation of Neural Correlates." *Cerebral Cortex* 27, no. 2 (2017): 1428–1438.

McEwen, B. S. 2017. "Neurobiological and Systemic Effects of Chronic Stress." *Chronic Stress (Thousand Oaks)*, January–December 2017. doi: 10.1177/2470547017692328

Meeks, T. W., and D. V. Jeste. "Neurobiology of Wisdom: A Literature Overview." *Archives of General Psychiatry* 66, no. 4 (2009): 355–365.

Osher, D., P. Cantor, J. Berg, L. Steyer, and T. Rose. "Drivers of Human Development: How Relationships and Context Shape Learning and Development." *Applied Developmental Science* 24, no. 1 (2020): 6–36.

Paul, A. M. *Origins: How the Nine Months before Birth Shape the Rest of Our Lives*. New York: Free Press, 2010.

Peters, J. C., and C. Kemner. "Facial Expressions Perceived by the Adolescent Brain: Towards the Proficient Use of Low Spatial Frequency Information." *Biological Psychology* 129 (2017): 1–7.

Plomin, R. *Behavioral Genetics in the Postgenomic Era*. Washington, D.C.: American Psychological Association, 2003.

Puderbaugh, M., and P. D. Emmady. "Neuroplasticity." *StatPearls*, 2022. https://www.statpearls.com/ArticleLibrary/viewarticle/97078

Ridley, M. *Genome: The Autobiography of a Species in 23 Chapters*. New York: HarperCollins, 1999.

Ridley, M. *Nature via Nurture: Genes, Experience, and What Makes Us Human*. New York: HarperCollins, 2003.

Rose, T. *The End of Average: How We Succeed in a World that Values Sameness*. New York: HarperOne, 2015.

Sapolsky, R. M. *Behave: The Biology of Humans at Our Best and Worst*. New York: Penguin, 2017.

Saxbe, D., L. Del Piero, M. H. Immordino-Yang, J. Kaplan, and G. Margolin. "Neural Correlates of Adolescents' Viewing of Parents' and Peers' Emotions: Associations with Risk-Taking Behavior and Risky Peer Affiliations." *Social Neuroscience* 10, no. 6 (2015): 592–604.

Shonkoff, J. P., A. S. Garner, Committee on Psychosocial Aspects Child and Family Health; Committee on Early Childhood, Adoption, and Dependent Care; Section on Developmental and Behavioral Pediatrics. "The Lifelong Effects of Early Childhood Adversity and Toxic Stress." *Pediatrics* 129, no. 1 (2012): e232–e246. doi: 10.1542/peds.2011-2663

Siegel, D. J. *Pocket Guide to Interpersonal Neurobiology: An Integrative Handbook of the Mind*. New York: Norton, 2012.

Stadelmann, C., S. Timmler, A. Barrantes-Freer, and M. Simons. "Myelin in the Central Nervous System: Structure, Function, and Pathology." *Physiological Reviews* 99, no. 3 (2019): 1381–1431.

Venkatraman, A., B. L Edlow, and M. H. Immordino-Yang. "The Brainstem in Emotion: A Review." *Frontiers in Neuroanatomy* 11 (2017): 15.

Voss, P., M. E. Thomas, J. M. Cisneros-Franco, and E. de Villers-Sidani. "Dynamic Brains and the Changing Rules of Neuroplasticity: Implications for Learning and Recovery." *Frontiers in Psychology* 8 (2017): 1657.

Xu, P., S. Peng, Y. J. Luo, and G. Gong. "Facial Expression Recognition: A Meta-Analytic Review of Theoretical Models and Neuroimaging Evidence." *Neuroscience & Biobehavioral Reviews* 127 (2021): 820–836.

CHAPTER 8

Cantor, P., R. M. Lerner, K. Pittman, P. A. Chase, and N. Gomperts. In Preparation. *Whole-Child Development and Thriving: A Dynamic Systems Approach.* NY: Cambridge University Press.

"Early Life Brain Architecture." Harvard Center on the Developing Child, 2021. https://developingchild.harvard.edu/science/key-concepts/brain-architecture/

Eagleman, D. *The Brain.* New York: Pantheon Books, 2015.

Frith, C. "Role of Facial Expressions in Social Interactions." *Philosophical Transactions of the Royal Society B: Biological Sciences* 364, no. 1535 (2009): 3453–3458.

Gopnik, A., A. N. Meltzoff, and P. K. Kuhl. *The Scientist in the Crib: Minds, Brains, and How Children Learn.* New York: William Morrow, 1999.

Hetherington, E. M., R. M. Lerner, M. Perlmutter, and Social Science Research Council (U.S.). *Child Development in Life-Span Perspective.* Hillsdale, N.J.: Erlbaum, 1988.

Keating, D. P. "Transformative Role of Epigenetics in Child Development Research: Commentary on the Special Section." *Child Development* 87, no. 1 (2016): 135–142.

Kim, P., and S. E. Watamura. *Two Open Windows: Infant and Parent Neurobiologic Change.* The Aspen Institute, 2015. https://ascend-resources.aspeninstitute.org/resources/two-open-windows-infant-and-parent-neurobiologic-change-2/

Landry, B. W., and S. W. Driscoll. "Physical Activity in Children and Adolescents." *Physical Medicine and Rehabilitation* 4, no. 11 (2012): 826–832.

Notterman, D. A., and C. Mitchell. "Epigenetics and Understanding the Impact of Social Determinants of Health." *Pediatric Clinics of North America* 62, no. 5 (2015): 1227–1240.

Parlato-Oliveira, E., C. Saint-Georges, D. Cohen, H. Pellerin, I. M. Pereira, C. Fouillet, M. Chetouani, M. Dommergues, and S. Viaux-Savelon. "'Motherese' Prosody in Fetal-Directed Speech: An Exploratory Study Using Automatic Social Signal Processing." *Frontiers in Psychology* 12 (2021): 646170. doi: 10.3389/fpsyg.2021.646170

Phillips, D. A., and A. E. Lowenstein. "Early Care, Education, and Child Development." *Annual Review of Psychology* 62 (2011): 483–500.

Siegel, D. J., and M. F. Solomon. *Mind, Consciousness, and Well-Being.* New York: Norton, 2020.

Swain, J. E., J. P. Lorberbaum, S. Kose, and L. Strathearn. 2007. "Brain Basis of Early Parent-Infant Interactions: Psychology, Physiology, and in vivo Functional Neuroimaging Studies." *Journal of Child Psychology and Psychiatry* 48, nos. 3-4 (2007): 262–287.

CHAPTER 9

Casey, B. J., R. M. Jones, and T. A. Hare. "The Adolescent Brain." *Annals of the New York Academy of Sciences* 1124 (2008): 111–126.

Chein, J., D. Albert, L. O'Brien, K. Uckert, and L. Steinberg. "Peers Increase Adolescent Risk Taking by Enhancing Activity in the Brain's Reward Circuitry." *Developmental Science* 14, no. 2 (2011): F1–F10.

Covey, S. *The 6 Most Important Decisions You'll Ever Make: A Guide for Teens.* New York: Simon & Schuster, 2011.

Harris, J. R. *The Nurture Assumption: Why Children Turn Out the Way They Do.* New York: Free Press, 2009.

Hetherington, E. M., R. M. Lerner, M. Perlmutter, and Social Science Research Council (U.S.). *Child Development in Life-Span Perspective.* Hillsdale, NJ: Erlbaum, 1988.

Hochberg, Z. E., and M. Konner. "Emerging Adulthood, a Pre-Adult Life-History Stage." *Frontiers in Endocrinology (Lausanne)* 10 (2019): 918.

Immordino-Yang, M. H., and D. R. Knecht. "Building Meaning Builds Teens' Brains." *ASCD* 77, no. 8 (2020).

Kreppner, K., and R. M. Lerner. *Family Systems and Life-Span Development.* Hillsdale, NJ: Erlbaum, 1989.

Kross, E., M. G. Berman, W. Mischel, E. E. Smith, and T. D. Wager. "Social Rejection Shares Somatosensory Representations with Physical Pain." *Proceedings of the National Academy of Sciences* 108, no. 15 (2011): 6270–6275.

Larsen, B., and B. Luna. "Adolescence as a Neurobiological Critical Period for the Development of Higher-Order Cognition." *Neuroscience & Biobehavioral Reviews* 94 (2018): 179–195.

Lerner, R. M. *The Developmental Science of Adolescence: History through Autobiography.* New York: Psychology Press, 2014.

Lerner, R. M., and L. E. Hess. *The Development of Personality, Self, and Ego in Adolescence.* Vol. 3. *Adolescence: Development, Diversity, and Context.* New York: Garland, 1999.

Lerner, R. M., and J. Jovanovic. *Cognitive and Moral Development and Academic Achievement in Adolescence.* Vol. 2. *Adolescence: Development, Diversity, and Context.* New York: Garland, 1999.

Lerner, R. M., and L. D. Steinberg. *Handbook of Adolescent Psychology*, 2nd ed. Hoboken, NJ: Wiley, 2004.

Malin, H., I. Liauw, and W. Damon. "Purpose and Character Development in Early Adolescence." *Journal of Youth and Adolescence* 46, no. 6 (2017): 1200–1215.

Romeo, R. D. "The Teenage Brain: The Stress Response and the Adolescent Brain." *Current Directions in Psychological Science* 22, no. 2 (2013): 140–145.

Saxbe, D., L. Del Piero, M. H. Immordino-Yang, J. Kaplan, and G. Margolin. "Neural Correlates of Adolescents' Viewing of Parents' and Peers' Emotions: Associations with Risk-Taking Behavior and Risky Peer Affiliations." *Social Neuroscience* 10, no. 6 (2015): 592–604.

Silbereisen, R. K., and R. M. Lerner. *Approaches to Positive Youth Development.* Los Angeles: Sage, 2007.

Steinberg, L. D. *Age of Opportunity: Lessons from the New Science of Adolescence.* Boston: Eamon Dolan/Houghton Mifflin Harcourt, 2014.

Steinberg, L. D. *Adolescence*, 12th ed. New York: McGraw-Hill Education, 2020.

Stixrud, W., and N. Johnson. *The Self-Driven Child: The Science and Sense of Giving Your Kids More Control over Their Lives.* New York: Viking Penguin, 2019.

Stixrud, W. R., and N. Johnson. *What Do You Say?: How to Talk with Kids to Build Motivation, Stress Tolerance, and a Happy Home.* New York: Viking, 2021.

Urban, T. "The Tail End," Wait but Why, December 11, 2015. https://waitbutwhy.com/2015/12/the-tail-end.html

CHAPTER 10

Bellis, M. A., K. Hardcastle, K. Ford, K. Hughes, K. Ashton, Z. Quigg, and N. Butler. "Does Continuous Trusted Adult Support in Childhood Impart Life-Course Resilience against Adverse Childhood Experiences—A Retrospective Study on Adult Health-Harming Behaviors and Mental Well-Being." *BMC Psychiatry* 17, no. 1 (2017): 110.

Bellis, M. A., K. Hughes, K. Ford, G. Ramos Rodriguez, D. Sethi, and J. Passmore. "Life Course Health Consequences and Associated Annual Costs of Adverse Childhood Experiences across Europe and North America: A Systematic Review and Meta-Analysis." *Lancet Public Health* 4, no. 10 (2019): e517–e528.

Bellis, M.A., K. Hughes, K. Ford, K. Hardcastle, C. Sharp, S. Wood, L. Homolova, and A. Davies. "Adverse Childhood Experiences and Sources of Childhood Resilience: A Retrospective Study of their Combined Relationships with Child Health and Educational Attendance." *BMC Public Health* 18 (2018): 792. doi.org/10.1186/s12889-018-5699-8

Bethell, C. D., N. Gombojav, and R. C. Whitaker. "Family Resilience and Connection Promote Flourishing among Us Children, Even Amid Adversity." *Health Affairs (Millwood)* 28, no. 5 (2019): 729–737.

Bronfenbrenner, U., and P. A. Morris. "The Bioecological Model of Human Development." In *Handbook of Child Psychology: Vol. 1. Theoretical Models of Human Development*, 6th ed., edited by R. M. Lerner, pp. 793–828. Hoboken, NJ: Wiley, 2006.

Brown, S. M., L. J. Schlueter, E. Hurwich-Reiss, J. Dmitrieva, E. Miles, and S. E. Watamura. "Parental Buffering in the Context of Poverty: Positive Parenting Behaviors Differentiate Young Children's Stress Reactivity Profiles." *Development and Psychopathology* 32, no. 5, (2020): 1778–1787.

Burke-Harris, N. *The Deepest Well: Healing the Long-Term Effects of Childhood Adversity*. New York: Mariner Books, 2018.

Buss, C., S. Entringer, N. K. Moog, P. Toepfer, D. A. Fair, H. N. Simhan, C. M. Heim, and P. D. Wadhwa. "Intergenerational Transmission of Maternal Childhood Maltreatment Exposure: Implications for Fetal Brain Development." *Journal of the American Academy of Child & Adolescent Psychiatry* 56, no. 5 (2017): 373–382.

Callina, K. S., S. K. Johnson, M. H. Buckingham, and R. M. Lerner. "Hope in Context: Developmental Profiles of Trust, Hopeful Future Expectations, and Civic Engagement across Adolescence." *Journal of Youth and Adolescence* 43, no. 6 (2014): 869–883.

Callina, K. S., S. K. Johnson, J. M. Tirrell, M. Batanova, M. B. Weiner, and R. M. Lerner. "Modeling Pathways of Character Development across the First Three Decades of Life: An Application of Integrative Data Analysis Techniques to Understanding the Development of Hopeful Future Expectations." *Journal of Youth and Adolescence* 46, no. 6 (2017): 1216–1237.

Cicchetti, D. "Resilience under Conditions of Extreme Stress: A Multilevel Perspective." *World Psychiatry* 93, no. 3 (2010): 145–154.

Clear, J. *Atomic Habits: Tiny Changes, Remarkable Results: An Easy and Proven Way to Build Good Habits and Break Bad Ones*. New York: Avery, 2018.

Bhushan, D. K. Kotz, J. McCall, S. Wirtz, R. Gilgoff, S. R. Dube, C. Powers, J. Olson-Morgan, M. Galeste, K. Patterson, L. Harris, A. Mills, C. Bethell, and N. Burke Harris. *Roadmap for Resilience: The California Surgeon General's Report on Adverse Childhood Experiences, Toxic Stress, and Health*, December 9, 2020. doi: 10.48019/PEAM8812

Fredrickson, B. L., and B. E. Kok. "Evidence for the Upward Spiral Stands Steady: A Response to Nickerson (2018)." *Psychological Science* 29, no. 3 (2018): 467–470.

Kelly, J. D. "Your Best Life: Breaking the Cycle: The Power of Gratitude." *Clinical Orthopaedics and Related Research* 474, no. 12 (2016): 2594–2597.

Kok, B. E., K. A. Coffey, M. A. Cohn, L. I. Catalino, T. Vacharkulksemsuk, S. B. Algoe, M. Brantley, and B. L. Fredrickson. "How Positive Emotions Build Physical Health: Perceived Positive Social Connections Account for the Upward Spiral between Positive Emotions and Vagal Tone." *Psychological Science* 24, no. 7 (2013): 1123–1132.

"Leading Causes of Death and Injury in the United States," Centers for Disease Control, 2022. https://www.cdc.gov/injury/wisqars/LeadingCauses.html

Lehrner, A., and R. Yehuda. "Trauma across Generations and Paths to Adaptation and Resilience." *Psychological Trauma* 10, no. 1 (2018): 22–29.

Merrick, M. T., D. C. Ford, K. A. Ports, and A. S. Guinn. "Prevalence of Adverse Childhood Experiences from the 2011–2014 Behavioral Risk Factor Surveillance System in 23 States." *JAMA Pediatrics* 172, no. 11 (2018): 1038–1044.

Merrick, M. T., D. C. Ford, K. A. Ports, . . . J. A. Mercy. *Vital Signs: Estimated Proportion of Adult Health Problems Attributable to Adverse Childhood Experiences and Implications for Prevention—25 States, 2015–2017. New York: Centers for Disease Control and Prevention*, 2019.

Neumann, I. D. "Oxytocin: The Neuropeptide of Love Reveals Some of Its Secrets." *Cell Metabolism* 5, no. 4 (2007): 231–233.

Park, C. L. "Meaning Making and Resilience." In *The Routledge International Handbook of Psychosocial Resilience* edited by U. Kumar, pp. 162–172. UK: Routledge/Taylor & Francis Group, 2017.

Plomin, R. "Genetics and Children's Experiences in the Family." *Journal of Child Psychology and Psychiatry* 36, no. 1 (1995): 33–68.

Racine, N., A. Plamondon, S. Madigan, S. McDonald, and S. Tough. "Maternal Adverse Childhood Experiences and Infant Development." *Pediatrics* 141, no. 4 (2018): e20172495. doi.org/10.1542/peds.2017-2495.

Schickedanz, A., N. Halfon, N. Sastry, and P. J. Chung. "Parents' Adverse Childhood Experiences and Their Children's Behavioral Health Problems." *Pediatrics* 142, no. 2 (2018): e20180023. doi: 10.1542/peds.2018-0023.

"The Search Institute: Developmental Relationships Framework." 2021. https://www.search-institute.org/developmental-relationships/developmental-relationships-framework/

Seshadri, K. G. "The Neuroendocrinology of Love." *Indian Journal of Endocrinology and Metabolism* 20, no. 4 (2016): 558–563.

Waldinger, R. J., and M. S. Schulz. "What's Love Got to Do with It? Social Functioning, Perceived Health, and Daily Happiness in Married Octogenarians." *Psychology and Aging* 25, no. 2 (2010): 422–431.

Wang, G., S. O. Walker, X. Hong, T. R. Bartell, and X. Wang. "Epigenetics and Early Life Origins of Chronic Noncommunicable Diseases." *Journal of Adolescent Health* 52, no. 2, Suppl. 2 (2013): S14–S21.

Wells, G. *The Ripple Effect: Sleep Better, Eat Better, Move Better, Think Better.* Toronto, Ontario: Collins, 2017.

CHAPTER 11

Csikszentmihalyi, M. "The Flow Experience." In D. Goleman and R. Davidson (Eds.), *Consciousness: Brain, States of Awareness and Mysticism.* New York: Harper & Row, 1979.

Loehr, J. E. *Athletic Excellence.* Denver: Forum, 1982.

Loehr, J. E. "The Ideal Performance State." *Sports Science Periodical on Research and Technology in Sport.* Addison-Wesley; January 1983.

Loehr, J. E. *Mental Toughness Training for Sports.* New York: Penguin, 1982.

Loehr, J. E., and J. Groppel. *The Corporate Athlete Advantage.* Orlando: Human Performance Institute, 2008.

Loehr, J. E., and T. Schwartz. "Making of a Corporate Athlete." *Harvard Business Review*, 2001.

Loehr, J. E., and T. Schwartz. *The Power of Full Engagement.* New York: Simon & Schuster, 2003.

Murphy, M., and R. White. *The Psychic Side of Sports.* Boston: Addison-Wesley, 1978.

Tohei, K. *Ki in Daily Life.* Tokyo: Ki No Kenkyukai H.O., 1980.

CHAPTER 12

Barrett, L. F. *How Emotions Are Made: The Secret Life of the Brain.* Boston: Houghton Mifflin Harcourt, 2017.

Barrett, L. F., K. A. Lindquist, and M. Gendron. "Language as Context for the Perception of Emotion." *Trends in Cognitive Sciences* 11 (2007): 327–332.

Barrett, L. F., B. Mesquita, K. N. Ochsner, and J. J. Gross. "The Experience of Emotion." *Annual Review of Psychology* 58 (2007): 373–403.

Bennett, M.P., and C. Lengacher. "Humor and Laughter May Influence Health: III. Laughter and Health Outcomes." *Evidence-Based Complementary and Alternative Medicine* 5 (2008): 37–40.

Boyatzis, R. E., D. Goleman, and K. Rhee. "Clustering Competence in Emotional Intelligence: Insights from the Emotional Competence Inventory (ECI)." In R. Bar-On and J. D. A. Parker (Eds.), *Handbook of Emotional Intelligence*, pp. 343–362. San Francisco: Jossey-Bass, 2000.

Boyce, T. W. *The Orchid and the Dandelion: Why Some Children Struggle and How All Can Thrive.* New York: Knopf, 2019.

Brackett, M. A., and S. E. Rivers. "Transforming Students' Lives with Social and Emotional Learning." In R. Pekrun and L. Linnenbrink-Garcia (Eds.), *International Handbook of Emotions in Education*, pp. 368–388. New York: Routledge, 2014.

Brackett, M. A., J. Patti, R. Stem, S. E. Rivers, N. A. Elbertson, C. Chisholm, and P. Salovey. "A Sustainable, Skill-Based Approach to Building Emotionally Literate Schools." In M. Hughes, H. L. Thompson, and J. B. Terrell (Eds.), *Handbook for Developing Emotional and Social Intelligence: Best Practices, Case Studies, and Strategies*, pp. 329–358. San Francisco: Pfeiffer/Wiley, 2009.

Brackett, M. *Permission to Feel: Unlocking the Power of Emotions to Help Our Kids, Ourselves, and Our Society Thrive*. New York: Celadon Books, 2019.

Bratton, V. K., N. G. Dodd, and F. W. Brown. "The Impact of Emotional Intelligence on Accuracy of Self-awareness and Leadership Performance." *Leadership & Organization Development Journal* 32 (2011): 127–149.

Brown, K. W., and R. M. Ryan. "The Benefits of Being Present: Mindfulness and Its Role in Psychological Well-Being." *Journal of Personality and Social Psychology* 84 (2003): 82–84.

Burg, J. M., and J. Michalak. "The Healthy Quality of Mindful Breathing: Associations with Rumination and Depression." *Cognitive Therapy and Research* 35 (2011): 179–185.

Burgdorf, J., and J. Panksepp. "The Neurobiology of Positive Emotions." *Neuroscience & Biobehavioral Reviews* 30 (2006): 173–187.

Cain, S. *Bittersweet: How Sorrow and Longing Make Us Whole*. New York: Crown, 2022

Clore, G. L., and J. R. Huntsinger. "How Emotions Inform Judgment and Regulate Thought." *Trends in Cognitive Sciences* 11 (2007): 393–399.

Cosmides, L., and J. Tooby. "Evolutionary Psychology and the Emotions." In M. Lewis and J. M. Haviland-Jones (Eds.), *Handbook of Emotions*, pp. 91–115. New York: Guilford Press, 2000.

Crum, J., M. Akinola, A. Martin, and S. Fath. "The Role of Stress Mindset in Shaping Cognitive, Emotional, and Physiological Responses to Challenging and Threatening Stress." *Anxiety, Stress, & Coping* 30 (2017): 379–395.

Crum, J., P. Salovey, and S. Achor. "Rethinking Stress: The Role of Mindsets in Determining the Stress Response." *Journal of Personality and Social Psychology* 104 (2013): 716–733.

Damasio, A. R. *Descartes' Error*. New York: Random House, 1995.

Danner, D. D., D. A. Snowdon, and W. V. Friesen. "Positive Emotions in Early Life and Longevity: Findings from the Nun Study." *Journal of Personality and Social Psychology* 80 (2001): 804–813.

Davidson, R. J., and S. Begley. *The Emotional Life of Your Brain: How Its Unique Patterns Affect the Way You Think, Feel, and Live—and How You Can Change Them*. London: Penguin, 2012.

Dweck, C. *Mindset: The New Psychology of Success*. New York: Ballantine Books, 2006.

Epel, E., A. A. Prather, E. Putennao, and A. J. Tomiyama. "Eat, Drink, and Be Sedentary: A Review of Health-Behaviors' Effects on Emotions and Affective States, and Implications for Interventions." In L. F. Barrett, M. Lewis, and J. M. Haviland-Jones (Eds.), *Handbook of Emotions*, pp. 685–706. New York: Guilford Press, 2016.

Forgas, J. P., and G. H. Bower. "Mood Effects on Person-Perception Judgments." In W. G. Parrott (Ed.), *Emotions in Social Psychology: Essential Readings*, pp. 204–215. Philadelphia: Psychology Press, 2001.

Forgas, J. P., and J. M. George. "Affective Influences on Judgments and Behavior in Organizations: An Information Processing Perspective." *Organizational Behavior and Human Decision Processes* 86 (2001): 3–34.

Fredrickson, B. L. "What Good Are Positive Emotions?" *Review of General Psychology* 2 (1998): 300–319.

Fredrickson, B. L. "Positive Emotions Broaden and Build." In P. Devine and A. Plant (Eds.), *Advances in Experimental Social Psychology*, vol. 47, pp. 1–53. Cambridge, MA: Academic Press, 2013.

Gainsburg, I., W. J. Sowden, B. Drake, W. Herold, and E. Kross. "Distanced Self-Talk Increases Rational Self-Interest." *Scientific Reports* 12, no. 2(2022): 511.

Gershon, M. D. *The Second Brain: The Scientific Basis of Gut Instinct and a Groundbreaking New Understanding of Nervous Disorders of the Stomach and Intestine*. New York: HarperCollins, 1998.

Genzel, B., J. R. D. Rarick, and P. A. Morris. "Stress and Emotion: Embodied, in Context, and across the Lifespan." In L. F. Barrett, M. Lewis, and J. M. Haviland-Jones (Eds.), *Handbook of Emotions*, pp. 707–735. New York: Guilford Press, 2016.

Goleman, D. *Emotional Intelligence: Why It Can Matter More Than IQ*. New York: Bantam Books, 1997.

Gross, J. J. "Emotion Regulation: Affective, Cognitive, and Social Consequences." *Psychophysiology* 39 (2002): 281–291.

Grossman, P., L. Niemann, S. Schmidt, and H. Walach. "Mindfulness-based Stress Reduction and Health Benefits: A Meta-Analysis." *Journal of Psychosomatic Research* 57 (2004): 35–43.

Heffernan, M., M. T. Griffin, and J. J. Fitzpatrick. "Self-Compassion and Emotional Intelligence in Nurses." *International Journal of Nursing Practice* 16 (2010): 366–373.

Huntsinger, J. R., L. M. Isbell, and G. L. Clore. "The Affective Control of Thought: Malleable, Not Fixed." *Psychological Review* 121 (2014): 600–618.

Immordino-Yang, M. H. *Emotions, Learning, and the Brain: Exploring the Educational Implications of Affective Neuroscience*. New York: Norton, 2015.

Isbell, L. M., and E. C. Lair. "Moods, Emotions, and Evaluations as Information." In D. Carlston (Ed.), *The Oxford Handbook of Social Cognition*, pp. 435–462. New York: Oxford University Press, 2013.

Isen, A. M., K. A. Daubman, and G. P. Nowicki. "Positive Affect Facilitates Creative Problem Solving." *Journal of Personality and Social Psychology* 52 (1987): 1122–1131.

Izard, C., E. M. Woodburn, K. J. Finlon, E. S. Krauthamer-Ewing, S. R. Grossman, and A. Seidenfeld. "Emotion Knowledge, Emotion Utilization, and Emotion Regulation." *Emotion Review* 3 (2011): 44–52.

Kabat-Zinn, J. *Full Catastrophe Living: Using the Wisdom of Your Body and Mind to Face Stress, Pain, and Illness*. New York: Delta, 1990.

Kross, E., and O. Ayduk. "Self-Distancing: Theory, Research, and Current Directions." In J. Olsen (Ed.), *Advances in Experimental Social Psychology*, vol. 55, pp. 81–136. Cambridge, MA: Academic Press, 2017

Kross, E., E. Bruehlman-Senecal, J. Park, A. Burson, A. Dougherty, H. Shablack, . . . O. Ayduk. "Self-Talk as a Regulatory Mechanism: How You Do It Matters." *Journal of Personality and Social Psychology* 106 (2014): 304–324.

LeDoux, J. "The Emotional Brain: The Mysterious Underpinnings of Emotional Life." *World and I* 12 (1997): 281–285.

Lerner, J. S., Y. Li, P. Valdesolo, and K. S. Kassam. "Emotion and Decision Making." *Annual Review of Psychology* 66 (2015): 799–823.

Lindquist, K. A., and L. F. Barrett. "A Functional Architecture of the Human Brain: Emerging Insights from the Science of Emotion." *Trends in Cognitive Sciences* 16 (2012): 533–540.

Lindquist, K. A., M. Gendron, and A. B. Satpute. "Language and Emotion: Putting Words into Feelings and Feelings into Words." In L. F. Barrett, M. Lewis, and J. M. Haviland-Jones (Eds.), *Handbook of Emotions*, pp. 579–594. New York: Guilford Press, 2016.

Martins, A., N. Ramalho, and E. Morin. "A Comprehensive Meta-Analysis of the Relationship between Emotional Intelligence and Health." *Journal of Personality and Individual Differences* 49 (2010): 554–564.

Mauss, I., S. Bunge, and J. J. Gross. "Automatic Emotion Regulation." *Social and Personality Psychology Compass* 1 (2007).

Mayer, J. D., P. Salovey, and D. R. Caruso. "Emotional Intelligence: Theory, Findings, and Implications." *Psychological Inquiry* 15 (2004): 197–215.

Mayer, J. D., and P. Salovey. "What Is Emotional Intelligence?" In P. Salovey, and D. Sluyter (Eds.). *Emotional Development and Emotional Intelligence: Implications for Educators*. New York: Basic Books, 1997.

Moon, T. W., and W. M. Hur. "Emotional Intelligence, Emotional Exhaustion, and Job Performance." *Social Behavior and Personality* 39 (2011): 1087–1096.

Moser, J. S., A. Dougherty, W. L. Mattson, B. Katz, T. P. Moran, D. Guevarra, and E. Kross. "Third-Person Self-Talk Facilitates Emotion Regulation without Engaging Cognitive Control: Converging Evidence from ERP and fMRI." *Scientific Reports* 7 (2017): 4519.

Nathanson, L., S. E. Rivers, L. M. Flynn, and M. A. Brackett. "Creating Emotionally Intelligent Schools with RULER." *Emotion Review 8* (2016): 305–310.

Oatley, K. D., and J. M. Jenkins. *Understanding Emotions*. Hoboken, NJ: Blackwell, 2018.

Pennebaker, J. W. "Putting Stress into Words: Health, Linguistic, and Therapeutic Implications." *Behavior Research and Therapy* 1 (1993): 539–548.

Pennebaker, J. W. "Expressive Writing in Psychological Science." *Perspectives on Psychological Science* 13 (2018): 226–229.

Petruzzello, S. J., D. M. Landers, B. D. Hatfield, K. A. Kubitz, and W. Salazar. "A Meta-Analysis on the Anxiety-Reducing Effects of Acute and Chronic Exercise." *Sports Medicine* 11 (1991): 143–182.

Rook, K. S. "Emotional Health and Positive versus Negative Social Exchanges: A Daily Analysis." *Applied Developmental Science* 5, no. 2 (2001): 86–97. doi .org/10.1207/S1532480XADS0502_4

Salovey, P., and J. D. Mayer. "Emotional Intelligence." *Imagination, Cognition, and Personality* 9 (1989): 185–211.

Schmeichel, B. J., and M. Inzlicht. "Incidental and Integral Effects of Emotions on Self-control." In M. D. Robinson, E. R. Watkins, and E. Harmon-Jones (Eds.), *Handbook of Cognition and Emotion*, pp. 272–290. New York: Guilford Press, 2013.

Schutte, N. S., J. M. Malouff, E. B. Thorsteinsson, N. Bhullar, and S. E. Rooke. "A Meta-Analytic Investigation of the Relationship between Emotional Intelligence and Health." *Personality and Individual Differences* 42 (2007): 921–933.

Zadra, J. R., and G. L. Clore. "Emotion and Perception: Role of Affective Information." *Wiley Interdisciplinary Reviews: Cognitive Science* 2, no. 6 (2011): 676–685. doi.org/10.1002/wcs.147.

CHAPTER 13

Allen, A. B., and M. R. Leary. "Self-Compassion, Stress, and Coping." *Social and Personality Psychology Compass* 4, no. 2 (2010): 107–118.

Astin, J. A. "Stress Reduction Through Mindfulness Meditation." *Psychotherapy and Psychosomatics* 66, no. 2 (1997): 97–106.

Benner, P., E. Roskies, and R. S. Lazarus. "Stress and Coping under Extreme Conditions." In J. E. Dimsdale (Ed.), *Survivors, Victims, and Perpetrators: Essays on the Nazi Holocaust*, pp. 219–258. Washington, DC: Hemisphere Press, 1980.

Black, D. S., and G. M. Slavich. "Mindfulness, Meditation and the Immune System: A Systematic Review of Randomized Controlled Trials." *Annals of the New York Academy of Sciences* 1373 (2016): 13–24.

Brown, K. W., and R. M. Ryan. "The Benefits of Being Present: Mindfulness and its Role in Psychological Well-Being." *Journal of Personality and Social Psychology* 84 (2003): 822–848.

Carlson, R. *Don't Sweat the Small Stuff . . . and It's All Small Stuff.* New York: Hachette, 1997.

Cassidy, T., M. McLaughlin, and M. Giles. "Benefit Finding in Response to General Life Stress: Measurement and Correlates." *Health Psychology and Behavioral Medicine* 2, no. 1 (2014): 268–282.

Cicchetti, D., and F. A. Rogosch. "Adaptive Coping Under Conditions of Extreme Stress: Multilevel Influences on the Determination of Resilience in Maltreated Children." *New Directions for Child and Adolescent Development* 124 (2009): 47–59.

Crum, A. "Evaluating a Mindset Training Program to Unleash the Enhancing Nature of Stress." *Academy of Management Proceedings*, no. 1, pp. 1–6. Briarcliff Manor, NY: Academy of Management, 2011.

Crum, A. J., P. Salovey, and S. Achor. "Rethinking Stress: The Role of Mindsets in Determining the Stress Response." *Journal of Personality and Social Psychology* 104 (2013): 716–733.

Crum, A. J., M. Akinola, A. Martin, and S. Fath. "The Role of Stress Mindset in Shaping Cognitive, Emotional, and Physiological Responses to Challenging and Threatening Stress." *Anxiety, Stress, & Coping* 30 (2017): 379–395.

Dweck, C. *Mindset: The New Psychology of Success.* New York: Random House, 2006.

Galef, J. *The Scout Mindset: Why Some People See Things Clearly and Others Don't.* New York: Penguin, 2021.

Gunderson, E. E., and R. H. Rahe. *Life Stress and Illness.* Springfield, IL: Charles C. Thomas, 1974.

Hofmann, S. G., S. Heering, A. T. Sawyer, and A. Asnaani. "How to Handle Anxiety: The Effects of Reappraisal, Acceptance, and Suppression Strategies on Anxious Arousal." *Behavior Research and Therapy* 47 (2009): 389–394.

Keller, A., K. Litzelman, L. E. Wisk, . . . W. P. Witt. "Does the Perception That Stress Affects Health Matter? The Association with Health and Mortality." *Health Psychology* 31, no. 5 (2011): 677–684. doi: 10.1037/a0026743

Khanna, M. S., and P. C. Kendall. *The Resilience Recipe: A Parent's Guide to Raising Fearless Kids in the Age of Anxiety*. Oakland, CA: New Harbinger, 2021.

Kobasa, S. C., S. R. Maddi, and S. Kahn. "Hardiness and Health: A Prospective Study." *Journal of Personality and Social Psychology* 42, no. 1 (1982): 168–177.

Kopin, I. "Adrenergic Responses Following Recognition of Stress." In S. Breznitz and O. Zinder (Eds.), *Molecular Biology of Stress*, vol. 97, pp. 123–132. New York: Alan R. Liss, 1989.

Kross, E., and O. Ayduk. "Self-Distancing Theory, Research, and Current Directions." In J. Olsen (Ed.), *Advances in Experimental Social Psychology*, vol. 55, pp. 81–136. Cambridge, MA: Academic Press, 2017.

Loehr, J. *Stress for Success*. New York: Random House, 1997.

Maddi, S. R. "The Courage and Strategies of Hardiness as Helpful in Growing Despite Major, Disruptive Stresses." *American Psychologist* 63, no. 6 (2008): 563–564.

McGonigal, K. *The Upside of Why Stress Is Good for You, and How to Get Good at It*. New York: Avery/Penguin Random House, 2015.

Moser, J. S., A. Dougherty, W. I. Mattson, B. Katz, T. P. Moran, D. Guevarra, . . . E. Kross. "Third-Person Self-Talk Facilitates Emotion Regulation without Engaging Cognitive Control: Converging Evidence from ERP and fMRI." *Scientific Reports* 7 (2017): 4519.

Neff, K. D. "The Development and Validation of a Scale to Measure Self-Compassion." *Self and Identity* 2, no. 3 (2003): 223–250.

Ostfeld, A. "The Role of Stress in Hypertension." *Journal of Human Stress* 5 (1979): 20.

Rutter, M. "Protective Factors in Children's Responses to Stress and Disadvantage." In M. Whalen and J. E. Rolfe (Eds.), *Primary Prevention of Psychopathology*, vol. 3, pp. 49–74. Hanover, NH: University Press of New England, 1979.

Seery, M. D., R. J. Leo, S. P. Lupien, C. L. Kondrak, and J. L. Almonte. "An Upside to Adversity? Moderate Cumulative Lifetime Adversity Is Associated with Resilient Responses in the Face of Controlled Stressors." *Psychological Science* 24, no. 7 (2013): 1181–1189.

Settipani, C., and P. C. Kendall. "The Effect of Child Distress on Accommodation of Anxiety: Relations with Maternal Beliefs, Empathy, and Anxiety." *Journal of Clinical Child and Adolescent Psychology* 46 (2017): 810–823.

Strohle, A. "Physical Activity, Exercise, Depression, and Anxiety Disorder." *Journal of Neural Transmission* 116 (2009): 777–784.

Twenge, J., T. Joiner, M. Rogers, and G. Martin. "Increases in Depressive Symptoms, Suicide-Related Outcomes, and Suicide Rates among U.S. Adolescents after 2010 and Links to Increased New Media Screen Time." *Clinical Psychological Science* 6 (2017): 3–17. doi:10.1177/2167702617723376.

Umberson, D., and J. Karas Montez. "Social Relationships and Health: A Flashpoint for Health Policy." *Journal of Health and Social Behavior* 51 (2010): S54–S66.

Wehner, M. "Talking to Yourself Isn't Crazy, It's a Stress Relief." *New York Post*, 2017.

Weiner, H. *Perturbing the Organism, The Biology of Stressful Experience.* Chicago: University of Chicago Press, 1992.

Weiss, J. M. "Effects of Coping Responses on Stress." *Journal of Comparative and Physiological Psychology* 65 (1968): 251–260.

Weiss, J. M., H. I. Glazer, L. A. Pohorecky, J. Brick, and N. E. Miller. "Effects of Chronic Exposure to Stressors on Avoidance-Escape Behavior and on Brain Norepinephrine." *Psychosomatic Medicine* 37 (1975): 522–533.

Zales, M. R. (Ed.) "The Concept of Stress in the Light of Studies on Disasters, Unemployment, and Loss: A Critical Analysis." *Stress in Health and Disease*, New York: Brunner/Mazel, 1985.

CHAPTER 14

Carli, M., A. Delle Fave, and F. Massimini. "The Quality of Experience in the Flow Channels: Comparison of Italian and U.S. Students." In M. Csikszentmihalyi and I. Csikszentmihalyi (Eds.), *Optimal Experience*, pp. 288–306. Cambridge, UK: Cambridge University Press, 1998.

Cooper, A. *Playing in the Zone: Exploring the Spiritual Dimensions of Sports.* Boston: Shambhala, 1998.

Csikszentmihalyi, M. *Beyond Boredom and Anxiety.* San Francisco: Jossey-Bass, 1975.

Csikszentmihalyi, M. *Attention and the Holistic Approach to Behavior.* Boston Springer, 1978.

Csikszentmihalyi, M. "Emergent Motivation and the Evolution of the Self." *Advances in Motivation and Achievement* 4 (1985): 93–119.

Csikszentmihalyi, M. "Reflection on Enjoyment." *Perspectives in Biology and Medicine* 28, no. 4 (1985): 489–497.

Csikszentmihalyi, M. *Flow.* New York: Harper Collins, 1990.

Csikszentmihalyi, M. *Finding Flow: The Psychology of Engagement with Everyday Life.* New York: Basic Books, 1997.

Csikszentmihalyi, M., and I. Csikszentmihalyi. *Optimal Experience*. Cambridge: Cambridge University Press, 1988.

Csikszentmihalyi, M., and R. Larson. "Intrinsic Rewards in School Crime." *Crime and Delinquency* 24 (1978): 322–335.

Csikszentmihalyi, M., and R. Larson. *Being Adolescent*. New York: Basic Books, 1984.

Csikszentmihalyi, M., and J. Lefevre. "Optimal Experience in Work and Leisure." *Journal of Personality and Social Psychology* 56 no. 5 (1989): 815–822.

Csikszentmihalyi, M., and J. Nakamura. "The Dynamics of Intrinsic Motivation: A Study of Adolescents." In R. Ames and C. Ames (Eds.), *Research on Motivation in Education: Goals and Cognitions*, pp. 45–71. New York: Academic Press, 1989.

Csikszentmihalyi, M., and J. Nakamura. "Emerging Goals and the Self-Regulation of Behavior." In R. S. Wyer (Ed.), *Advances in Social Cognition. Perspectives on Behavioral Self-Regulation*, vol. 12, pp. 107–118. Mahwah, NJ: Erlbaum, 1999.

Csikszentmihalyi, M., and K. Rathunde. "The Measurement of Flow in Everyday Life." *Nebraska Symposium on Motivation* 40 (1993): 57–97.

Csikszentmihalyi, M., and R. Robinson. *The Art of Seeing*. Malibu, CA: J. Paul Getty Museum and the Getty Center for Education in the Arts, 1990.

Csikszentmihalyi, M., K. Rathunde, and S. Whalen. *Talented Teenagers*. Cambridge, UK: Cambridge University Press, 1993.

Deci, E. *Intrinsic Motivation*. New York: Plenum Press, 1975.

Deci, E. L., and R. M. Ryan. *Intrinsic Motivation and Self-Determination in Human Behavior*. New York: Plenum Press, 1985.

Gallwey, W. T. *The Inner Game of Tennis*. London: Pan Books, 1974.

Gould, D. "Goal Setting for Peak Performance." In J. M. Williams (Ed.), *Applied Sport Psychology: Personal Growth to Peak Performance*, 3rd ed, pp. 182–196. Mountain View, CA: Notion Press, 1998.

Hektner, J., and K. Asakawa. "Learning to Like Challenges." In M. Csikszentmihalyi and B. Schneider (Eds.), *Becoming Adult*, pp. 95–112. New York: Basic Books, 2000.

Hektner, J., and M. Csikszentmihalyi. "A Longitudinal Exploration of Flow and Intrinsic Motivation in Adolescents." Paper presented at the annual meeting of the American Educational Research Association, New York, 1996.

Herrigel, E. *Zen and the Art of Archery*. New York: Vintage Books, 1953.

Jackson, S. A. "Toward a Conceptual Understanding of the Flow Experience in Elite Athletes." *Research Quarterly for Exercise and Sport* 67, no. 1 (1996): 76–90.

Jackson, S. A., J. C. Kimiecik, S. Ford, and H. W. Marsh. "Psychological Correlates of Flow in Sport." *Journal of Sport and Exercise Psychology* 20 (1998): 358–378.

Jackson, S. A., and G. C. Roberts. "Positive Performance States of Athletes: Toward a Conceptual Understanding of Peak Performance." *Sport Psychologist* 6, no. 2 (1992): 156–171.

Kubey, R., and M. Csikszentmihalyi. *Television and the Quality of Life.* Hillsdale, NJ: Erlbaum, 1990.

Maslow, A. *Toward a Psychology of Being,* 2nd ed. New York: van Nostrand Reinhold, 1968.

Mayers, P. "Flow in Adolescence and Its Relation to School Experience." *Dissertation Abstracts International Section A: Humanities and Social Sciences* 39 (1-A), (1978): 197–198.

Murphy, S., and R. A. White. *In the Zone: Transcendent Experience in Sports.* New York: Penguin, 1994.

Rathunde, K. "Parent—Adolescent Interaction and Optimal Experience." *Journal of Youth and Adolescence* 26, no. 6 (1997): 669–689.

Chapter 15

Armstrong, D. *Managing by Storying Around: A New Method of Leadership.* New York: Doubleday, 1982.

Baldwin, C. *Storycatcher: Making Sense of Our Lives through the Power and Practice of Story.* New York: New World Library, 2007.

Bateson, M. C. *Composing a Life.* New York: Grove Press, 2001.

Baumeister, R. F. *Meanings of Life.* New York: Guilford Press, 1991.

Brown, J. S., S. Denning, K. Groh, and L. Prusak. *Storytelling in Organizations: Why Storytelling Is Transforming 21st Century Organizations and Management.* New York: Routledge, 2005.

Bruner, J. "The 'Remembered' Self." In U. Neisser and R. Fivush (Eds.), *The Remembering Self: Construction and Accuracy in the Self-Narrative.* Cambridge, UK: Cambridge University Press, 1994.

Crossley, M. L. *Introducing Narrative Psychology: Self-Trauma, and the Construction of Meaning.* Philadelphia: Open University Press, 2000.

Denning, S. *The Leader's Guide to Storytelling: Mastering the Art and Discipline of Business Narrative.* Hoboken, NJ: Wiley, 2005.

Eakin, P. J. *How Our Lives Become Stories.* Ithaca, NY: Cornell University Press, 2019.

Gabriel, Y. *Storytelling in Organizations: Facts, Fictions, and Fantasies*. Oxford, UK: Oxford University Press, 2000.

Hammack, P. L. "Narrative and the Cultural Psychology of Identity." *Personality and Social Psychology Review* 12, no. 3 (2008): 222–247.

Howard, G. S. *A Tale of Two Stories: Excursions into a Narrative Approach to Psychology*. Notre Dame, IN: Academic Publications, 1989.

Ibarra, H. *Working Identity: Unconventional Strategies for Reinventing Your Career*. Boston: Harvard Business Press, 2004.

Jill, M. S. W., and G. Combs. *Narrative Therapy: The Social Construction of Preferred Realities*. New York: Norton, 1996.

Josselson, R. "Imaging the Real: Empathy, Narrative, and the Dialogic Self." In R. Josselson and A. Lieblich (Eds.), *The Narrative Study of Lives*, vol. 3, pp. 27–44. Thousand Oaks, CA: Sage, 1995.

Leonard, G., and M. Murphy. *The Life We Are Given*. New York: Tarcher/Putnam, 1995.

Lipman, D. *Improving Your Storytelling*. Little Rock, AR: August House, 1999.

Loehr, J. *The Power of Story: Change Your Story, Change Your Destiny in Business and in Life*. New York: Free Press, 2008.

Maguire, J. *The Power of Personal Storytelling*. New York: Penguin Putnam, 1988.

McAdams, D. P. "The Psychology of Life Stories." *Review of General Psychology* 5 (2001): 100–122.

McAdams, D. *Power, Intimacy and the Life Story*. New York: Guilford Press, 1988.

McAdams, D. *The Stories We Live By*. New York: Guilford Press, 1993.

McKee, R. *Story*. New York: Regan Books, 1997.

Mishler, E. G. "Models of Narrative Analysis: A Typology." *Journal of Narrative and Life History* 5 (1995): 87–123.

Monk, G., J. Winslade, K. Crocket, and D. Epton. *Narrative Therapy in Practice*. San Francisco: Jossey-Bass, 1997.

Rosenwald, G. C., and R. L. Ochberg (Eds.). *Storied Lives: The Cultural Politics of Self-Understanding*. New Haven, CT: Yale University Press, 1992.

Russell, R. L., and J. Lucariello. "Narrative, Yes: Narrative ad Infinitum, No!" *American Psychologist* 47 (1992): 671–672.

Sarbin, T. R. (Ed.). *Narrative Psychology: The Storied Nature of Human Conduct*. New York: Praeger, 1986.

Sawyer, R. *The Way of the Storyteller*. New York: Penguin Books, 1976.

Simmons, A. *The Story Factor*. New York: Basic Books, 2001.

Taylor, S. *Positive Illusions*. New York: Basic Books, 1989.

Weinstein, A. *Recovering Your Story*. New York: Random House, 2006.

White, M. *Re-Authoring Lives: Interviews & Essays*. Adelaide, Australia: Dulwich Centre, 1995.

Chapter 16

Adams, J. S., A. Tashchian, and T. H. Shore. "Codes of Ethics as Signals for Ethical Behavior." *Journal of Business Ethics* 29, no. 3 (2001): 199–211.

Baker, D., . . . K. B. Sorenson. "Guidebook to Decision-Making Methods." Developed for the Department of Energy, WSRC-IM-2002-00002, December 2001. https://www.researchgate.net/publication/255621095 _Guidebook_to_Decision-Making_Methods

Carver, C. S. "Self-Awareness." In M. R. Leary and J. P. Tangney (Eds.), *Handbook of Self and Identity*, pp. 59–68. New York: Guilford Press, 2012.

De Smet, A., G. Jost, and L. Weiss. "Three Keys to Faster, Better Decisions." *McKinsey Quarterly* (May 1, 2019).

Fogg, B. J. *Tiny Habits: The Small Changes that Change Everything*. Boston: Houghton Mifflin Harcourt, 2019.

Hammond, J. S., R. L. Keeney, and H. Raiffa. *Smart Choice: A Practical Guide to Making Better Decisions*. Boston: Harvard Business School Press, 1999.

Latham, A. "12 Reasons Why How You Make Decisions Is More Important Than What You Decide." *Forbes*, 2015.

Rea, P. J., J. K. Stoller, and A. Kolp. *Exception to the Rule: The Surprising Science of Character-based Culture, Engagement, and Performance*. New York: McGraw Hill Professional, 2018.

Chapter 17

Bazerman, M. H. *Better, Not Perfect: A Realist's Guide to Maximum Sustainable Goodness*. New York: HarperCollins, 2020.

Holiday, R. *The Obstacle Is the Way: The Timeless Art of Turning Trials into Triumph*. New York: Penguin, 2014.

Loehr, J. *The Only Way to Win: How Building Character Drives Higher Achievement and Greater Fulfillment in Business and Life*. London: Hachette UK, 2012.

Loehr, J., and C. Kenny. *Leading with Character: 10 Minutes a Day to a Brilliant Legacy Set*. Hoboken, NJ: Wiley, 2020.

Strecher, V. *Life on Purpose: How Living for What Matters Most Changes Everything*. New York: HarperCollins, 2016

CHAPTER 18

Associated Press, "Easily Obtained Steroids Focus of Sports Debate." *Star News Online*, November 29, 2003. https://www.starnewsonline.com/story/news/2003/11/30/easily-obtained-steroids-focus-of-sports-debate/30532684007/

Goldman, B., R. Klatz, and P. J. Bush. "Death in the Locker Room." Chicago: Elite Sports Medicine Publications, 1992.

ACKNOWLEDGMENTS

JIM'S ACKNOWLEDGMENTS

My first and most important teachers of decision-making were my parents, Mary and Con. It is my sincere hope that I would be for my three sons, Michael, Patrick, and Jeffrey, what my parents were for me. Other powerful influencers are my sister, Jane (Sister Margaret Mary), and my brother, Tom. I am immensely grateful to all of these teachers, as I still have much to learn.

To Sheila Ohlsson, you have been a joy to collaborate with and a treasure trove of insights in writing this book. You are authentic, innovative, humble, and brilliant.

To my longtime friend and business partner for over 30 years, Dr. Jack Groppel, thank you!

To Pat Loehr, John Collingwood, Caren Kenney, and Peter Scaturro, for their help with this manuscript.

To Dan Ritchie, for preparing such an extraordinary foreword.

To Sally Baker, Debbie Schindler, Amy Handy, and all the Wiley support staff who helped make this book possible. It has been a joy working with you all.

To all the current and former Human Performance Institute staff, of whom I am so proud, especially Sandy Friedrich, Chris Osorio, Fred Harburg, Chris Jordan, Bill McAlpine, Jenny Susser, Theresa Robinson, Jenn George, Lynn Seth, Jill Sharp, Cindy Heroux, Jenny Evans, Renate Gaisser, Stacey Sullivan, Phil Black, Tara Collingwood, Raphaela O'Day, Paul Wylie, Chris and Kara Mohr, Phil Burton, Natalie Johnson, Bob Carr, Bill Donovan, Steve Page, Lorenzo Beltrame, Raquel Garzon, Caroline Rivera, Becky Hoholski, Mike Florence, Greg Lieberman, Kevin Morris, Joy Norton, Sharon Helgerud, Dwayne Wright, Rhonda Waters, Steve and Jessalaynn Bush, Diane Nisbett, Tim Walker, Melissa Scott, Greg Grazen, Jenn Lea,

Brenda Ranero, Chris Allredge, Emily Lewinger, Aileen Teira, Bruce Highfield, Lesandra Hale, Sarah Wallgren, Brian Ballay, Ashley Meyers, Cheryl Branciforte, Kirsten Westlund, Jennifer Turgiss, Francene Mitchell, Jennifer Bruno, Cat and Jessica Bradu, Lindsey Brooks, Ignacio Monsalve, Ignacio and Elizabeth Esperanza, and Taisha Ramseur.

To all the clients who have touched my life and helped form the basis of my thinking, and to the countless thought leaders and researchers who have inspired this work.

To Tom and Shaun Gulliksen, Coach Guy Gibbs, Barbara Schulte, Chip Bergh, George Dom, Ray Smith, Tom Davin, David and Kelly Leadbetter, Jim and Susanna Courier, Brian Park, Peter Fasolo, Kevin Wildenhaus, Vic Strecher, Dan and Karen Jansen, Pat Van der Meer, Dan Santorum, Jorge Andrew, Julie Jilly, Louie and Helma Cap, Roy Barth, John Evert, Kirk Spahn, Monica Seles, Jay Senter, Mike Mackinzie, Chris Abate, John Embree, Doug MacCurdy, Renee Heckler, Lee DeYoung, Luis Mediero, Emilio Sanchez, Arantxa Sanchez Vicario, Tore and Eddie Rasavage, Anni Miller, Paul and Penny Hancock, Maggie Borer, Paul and Kathy Lubbers, Randy Gerber, Carey and Helen Bos, Matt Turner, Bill and Mary Rompf, Amy Wishingrad, Coach Billy Donovan, Brett Ledbetter, Jeff and Sherri Sklar, Fritz Nau, Walker and Ray Sahag, Tom Prichard, Stephen M.R. Covey, Lester Gruda, Gloria Caulfield, Virginia Savage, Cheryl Jenson, Meggan Hill-McQueeney, Brett Hobden, Amy Vest, Ethan Lin, Mike Wang, and Kelsey Abergel, for your friendship and unwavering support.

To Pat Loehr, for his creative illustrations and tireless work with the manuscript of this book, and to Jennifer Loehr, Christy Loehr, Keli Loehr, and C J Loehr for being such extraordinary mothers.

Finally, and most importantly, to four extraordinary human beings, Vickie Zoellner, Gordon Uehling, Michael Rouse, and Walter Buckley, for continuing to inspire me to pursue my dream.

SHEILA'S ACKNOWLEDGMENTS

Thank you to my father, the late Dr. John Ohlsson, from whom I inherited a fascination with biological science, a lifelong love of learning, and an endless curiosity about how people develop into who they are.

And to my mother, Mariza Ohlsson, who showed me what grit, perseverance, and resilience look like, and who taught me the importance of prioritizing health and wellness, which has served as the bedrock for all I've been able to do in life.

Jack, Charlie, and Wyatt, you are the center of my universe. I love you to the moon and back, and always will! I hope our book provides you with hope, inspiration, and a roadmap to live your healthiest, happiest, and most meaningful lives. To Willy, thank you for being a wonderful father to our boys, and for the decisions you've made across time to challenge yourself and nurture your own personal growth. And to my amazing parents-in-law, Diana and Mallory Walker, you've been there for me through thick and thin, and I am grateful for you!

I'd like to thank my extraordinary co-author Dr. Jim Loehr, whose friendship, mentorship, wisdom, humility, generosity, kindness, and wry, clever and downright nutty sense of humor have helped me grow both personally and professionally in ways words can't describe. Suffice to say, writing this book with you was a transformative life experience and an indescribable gift! Thanks too to Pat Loehr, whose brilliance in graphic design helped bring our ideas to life. Thinking and creating with you two was a rich off-road adventure of epic proportions!

To Dan Ritchie, you are a soul mate friend and true hero to me. You embody what wise decision-making looks like in real life, how health comes first 24/7 and 365 days a year. You are a living example of our shared Y.O.D.A. code of Kindness, Gratitude, Generosity, Integrity, Humility, and Courage. Thank you for believing in me, and for always, always showing up. You inspire me and are my True North for who I want to be when I grow up.

To Sally Baker, Debbie Schindler, Amy Handy, and the fabulous team at Wiley—thank you for making our book possible. It has been a joy and an honor to work with you!

Thank you to the wonderful friends and colleagues who provided thoughtful feedback on the manuscript: Dr. Marc Brackett, Dr. Mary Helen Immordino-Yang, Dr. Bill Stixrud, Ned Johnson, David Thomson, Dr. Ethan Kross, Kaja Perina, Jim Courier, Dr. Shelly Smith-Acuna, Dr. Brian Gearity, Priscilla Scobie, Dr. Rand Harrington, Glenn Whitman, and Gary Makar.

To my amazing high school and college-aged reviewers, Jack Walker, Charlie Walker, Annalee Miner, Lily D'Hondt, Ike Eastman, and Matthew Gettachew. In the end, this book is for *you*, intended to support you in living your best possible lives, setting the stage to make the kinds of thoughtful and wise decisions that help you flourish and achieve your dreams. Activate your Y.O.D.A. code early in life and go shine your extraordinary light into our world!

My deepest gratitude for the magnificent human beings who, across time, have provided the inspiration, ideas, belief, kindness, and support that have both sustained me and helped make the seemingly impossible feel legitimately possible. Thank you to Jamie Lee Curtis, Justin Sherman, Jackie Merrill, Katharine Weymouth, Dr. Joan Borysenko, Pirie Jones Grossman, Dr. Sasha Heinz, Stephanie Perenchio, Diana Kapp, Jan Aronson, Shirley Turteltaub, Rhea Turteltaub, Jennifer Noland, Allyn Stewart, Tim Wolff, Drew Daly, Mary Murphy, Dr. Joe Belanoff, Claire Shipman, Heather Mulvihill, Merrell Cherouny, Dr. Maxine Isaacs, Colleen Daly, Susan LaSalla, Carrie Trinh, Neal and Chie Ohlsson, Karen Ehrman, Dr. Paula Grissom, Helen Thorpe, Mary Clark, Dr. Jeremy Haefner, Mark Nealon, Dr. Joanne Steinwachs, Deb Mahan, Dr. Suzanne Schimmel, Dr. Annie Moore, Dr. Sona Dimidjian, Chris Davenport, George Karl, Brett Goldberg, Oyvind Gulbrandson, Kristin McKissick, Melissa Thomas, Sarah Hirshland, Charlie Huebner, Dr. Chip Benight, Barb Grogan, Lauren Casteel, Jim Collins, Mel Rutty, Lynn Hill, Sara Gebre, Gruffie Clough, Darcey Brown, Dr. Norma Brooks, the late Dr. David Hamburg, Anna Deavere Smith, Gail Larsen, Linda Smith, Dr. Maria Velleca Donoghue, Dr. Carol Ludwig, Dr. Pam Cantor, Bethany Little, Dr. Lee Savio Beers, Laura Slover, Gina Coburn, Kirtsten Lodal, Michele Jolin, the late Marilyn Glosserman, Mike Glosserman, Rocio Sallum Speets, Katherine Bradley, Jen Klein, Linda Potter, Dr. Tim Shriver, Alfred Moses, Dr. Susan Wechsler, Carole Ranney, Lou Stovall, Jennifer Brown Lerner, Tom Farrey, Val Kondos-Field, Paul Tough, Leela Rao Ellis, Liza and Raz Ingrasci, Michael Gervais, Dr. Andrea Ettekal, Dr. Jen Agans, Dr. Mary Arnold, Dr. Amanda Visek, Joseph Itaya, Dr. Robin Stern, Helen Churko, Arthur Sulzberger, Jr., Paul Carttar, Vesa Ponkka, Ron Smarr, Jan Shelburne, Simmy Pell, Shelagh Meehan, Andrea Rice, Pat Delaney,

Diana Kitt, Jeanne Swiacki, Louise Gengler, Caryn Krasner, Rhona Kaczmarek, Diane Schayes, Fritz and Mary Lynn Garger, Dan Levin, Sherrie Farris, and the beautiful Bonnie Gibson.

Each of you, in your own right, is a model of wise decision-making, kindness, humanity, and humility. Friendship is the medicine of life, and I draw upon experiences over the years from each of you. Whether hitting tennis balls, climbing mountains, dreaming about big ideas, or engaged in free-flow conversation sharing the details of our lives, I simply can't say how grateful I am for your presence and unwavering support.

To the generous mentors who supported my nonlinear pivot out of finance and into academia: Dr. Robert Plomin at King's College London at the Social, Genetic and Developmental Psychiatry Centre; Dr. Deborah Phillips at Georgetown University; Dr. Xiaobin Wang and Dr. Bob Blum at the Johns Hopkins Bloomberg School of Public Health; Dr. Mariale Hardiman at the Johns Hopkins School of Education; Dr. Doug Granger at the University of California, Irvine; and Dr. Rich Lerner at Tufts University. As well, my gratitude to the amazing Dr. Sachiko Kuno for honoring me with a fellowship that marked the official start of the chapter I'm in now: making complex biosocial science understandable and practical, to help people live their healthiest and best possible lives. I count my lucky stars to have found each and every one of you, brought together by inexplicable synchronicity. I strive daily to make you proud for having taken a chance on me.

To the team at the Youth Performance Institute, you inspire me and I'm deeply grateful to be a part of the family. Thank you to Vickie Zoellner, Gordon Uehling, Buck Buckley, Michael Rouse, Amy Vest, Ethan Lin, Mike Wang, and Kelsey Abergel. May we go out and make our world a healthier, kinder, more purposeful and loving place for all!

Finally, to my Y.O.D.A. advisory board: You know who you are. Your names are scattered throughout this section, and I simply cannot imagine my life journey without you. Thank you for always making me feel seen, heard, valued, and understood, no matter what the circumstances. The African term *Ubuntu*, loosely translated, means "I am me because you are you," and it is solely because of you, and who I get to be when I am with you, that my contribution to this book was possible.

INDEX